In his books, films and lectures, Thomas Sheridan outlines—in layman and direct language—an introductory approach to behaviourism, myth, perception, archetypes, neuroscience, psychology and pathology, in order to explain the nature and methodology of the puzzling people and the puzzling situations which make the world such a bewildering and traumatic place at times. These books are considered field guides for social and psychological well-being, leading towards ultimately surviving and thriving in a world of engineered chaos and mass hysteria.

www.thomassheridanarts.com

*This Book is Dedicated to the Victims of Religious
and Political Fanatics Everywhere.*

*For They Who Attack Freedom of Speech,
Do So From the Prison of Their Own Minds.*

Walpurgis Night

Volume One 1919 - 1933

Thomas Sheridan

First Edition

Published by Thomas Sheridan Arts
First Edition
thomassheridanarts.com

ISBN: 978-1-291-81824-6

Includes Original Artwork by Thomas Sheridan

Copyright 2014

All Rights Reserved. No part of this publication may be reproduced, stored in a retrieval system, or transmitted in any form or by any means, electronic, mechanical, photocopying, recording or otherwise, without the prior permission of the copyright owner.

This is a Never-for-Kindle Book

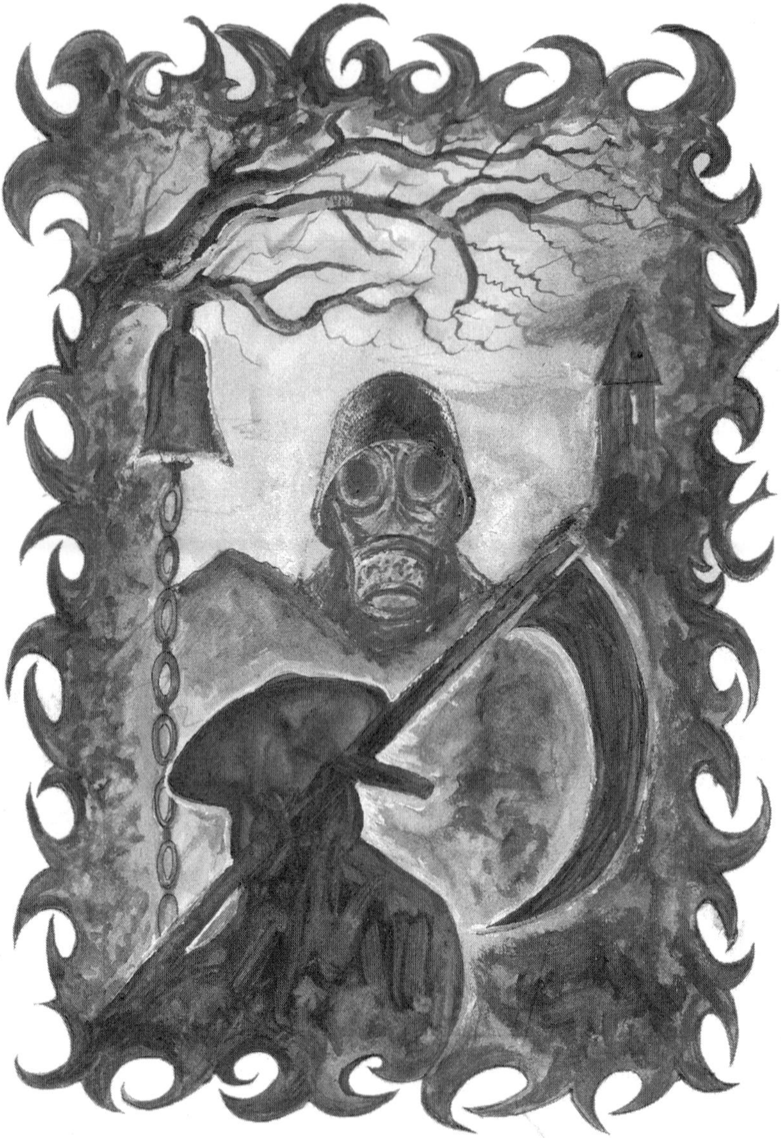

INTRODUCTION

In 1913, Carl Jung, the Swiss psychoanalyst and artist, had a terrifying vision on the eve of the Great War (1914-18), predicting what lay in wait for Europe, along with the chain reaction it would unleash upon the human psyche as a whole. In October of that year, while Jung was out travelling, he was overcome by a paralysing vision in which he witnessed a tsunami covering all of northern and low-lying Europe that would eventually turn into an ocean of human blood. This vision lasted about one hour. Years later, he wrote, "As a human being he may have moods and a will and personal aims, but as an artist he is "man" in a higher sense—he is "collective man"—one who carries and shapes the unconscious, psychic forms of mankind." What Jung was describing was the almost supernatural ability of artists to predict the future as powerful symbolic events of important synchronicities which are undeniable in their meaning.

The reason for this may lie in the mysterious asymmetry of the human brain, whereby artists tend to develop a kind of 'background vision', which allows a more noetic and intuitive insight into the collective unconscious of the human condition. A condition that binds us all at the subconscious level and exists outside the realities of space and time. Thus, artists appear to have an allegorical future vision, which is then presented in the form of symbolic creative works which reveal their prophetic nature when the actual event(s) arrive. This is one of the primary reasons why artists are so highly sought after by popes and politicians, as well as by Wall Street and Madison Avenue advertising agencies: in order for the Lords of Perception to cast their future realities forward in time, rather than allow artists to present the future before anyone else is aware of on-coming events. Hence, why ritual magic was known for hundreds of years simply as 'The Art'.

On the day that Adolf Hitler was born, Friedrich Nietzsche is reported to have written, "I know my fate. One day my name will be associated with the memory of something tremendous—a crisis without equal on earth, the most profound collision of conscience, a decision that was conjured up against everything that had been believed, demanded, hallowed so far."

Around the same time period, when Adolf Hitler's mother was about to deliver her son, the German *Symbolist/Art Nouveau* painter Franz von Stuck was working on a painting entitled *Die Wilde Jagd* (Wild Chase), portraying a vicious image of Wotan, the Teutonic god of death and destruction. The mad night hunter who leaves horror and mayhem in his wake—bearing an uncanny resemblance to the adult Adolf Hitler—complete with forelock over the left temple, intense eyes and even a small moustache amidst a landscape of ravished women and scattered corpses. Later, it was to become one of Adolf Hitler's favourite paintings, along with another painting by von Stuck, of *Medusa*, bearing an uncanny resemblance to Hitler's mother, Klara.

Artists can, if they allow themselves to be subjected to the muse, ostensibly become 'intuitive magicians', as their creative intention can, at times, act as an oracle or conduit between various forms and layers of the collective unconscious. Richard Wagner, William Blake and George Orwell would be examples of artists who were intuitive magicians. They acted as beacons—both altruistic and pathological —in relation to changing and on-coming turbulent dynamics within human consciousness. I myself have experienced this artistic 'divination' with some of my own art. However, along with this often unrecognised ability, the artist can also be co-opted as a useful conduit whereby pathological forms of consciousness try to seize the artist's creative intention in order to ravage and disrupt human consciousness within the five sense reality.

Personally speaking, until 2012 I had no firm belief in the supernatural beyond a fortean inquisitive interest. I have long been fascinated by the paranormal, yet did not accept it as anything other than the dynamics of the universe we have yet to fully understand. In May 2012, while I was working on a painting and researching for this book—specifically, in regards to the events in Munich in 1919— I was overcome with what I can only term as a sense of 'pure evil' trying to murder me. A sensation so toxic that I started painting an image of an alien 'ghost' rising above Munich in 1919, which felt as if it was literally draining my life energy out through my feet as I painted it. It was the most terrifying experience, and I do not say this lightly, having witnessed the horrific effects of a car bomb in Dublin as a child in the 1970s.

Only by dragging myself out of my art studio could I escape the sensation of sheer dread. It took me days to recover, and when I eventually returned to the studio, everything was normal again. I have no idea what took place, but I never want to experience it ever again. Evil—whatever evil is—is a real force in the universe, and it has a hatred for all humanity, and is especially hateful towards creative individuals. At the risk of sounding narcissistic, it was as if I was being warned not to tackle this topic. It was as if I was not meant to study this period of history and present this information within the framework of my own work on collective psychopathology and control of human perceptions. The event had the opposite effect; I was determined to continue on with this work. I found myself, in the months ahead, 'attacked', from all quarters; from religious and political fanatics who sought to destroy my work into psychopathology within the corridors of power, to being harassed by random and clearly unstable individuals with harassing emails and phone calls. This also included bizarre and easily disproven accusations being made by politically connected individuals with a long history of repeatedly doing the same to progressive activists and researchers.

It was as if something beyond this level of consciousness had mobilised their foot soldiers within this five sense reality of human consciousness to silence me before I could embark on this project and present it according to my own perception of the events which took place within the human psyche during the last one hundred and fifty years, and in particular, the spells cast upon humanity since 1919; a year which I believe is far more pivotal to understanding the world we live in than the years 1984, 2001 or any other year between now and 2020.

In my opinion, the significance of 1919 has been played down for this very reason. The psychotic and psychopathic attacks which I had been subjected to on the eve of this project told me that I was meant to complete this work due to the fact that as I persevered, numerous new doors and opportunities opened before me. It seems that there were two teams playing this game. Within weeks of my strange and terrifying experience, I was researching German movies made at the time of the Weimar Republic, and in particular, films produced during 1919. I came across a movie directed by Robert Reinert entitled *Nerven* (Nerves), made during that very year. The film dealt with the psychological and emotional torment of ordinary Germans as they experienced these sensations during 1919. What made this discovery so remarkable to me was that the original poster produced for the movie featured the image of the same 'alien ghost' that I had painted in my studio during what I can only term a 'psychic attack'. To my recollection, I had not previously seen this specific movie poster, and I was completely unaware of the existence of the movie *Nerven*. Yet I have painted the unfinished image of the 'demon' from the *Nerven* poster almost verbatim (see following page over).

The world is a far more 'magical' place than we are told and taught about in school, or that which is spoken of within mainstream media.

The people who are in control of this planet—both psychopathic, along with well meaning bureaucrats—are the repository of bizarre and occult forces functioning through the dynamics of their own consciousness. Some know it; most do not. There are 'useful idiots' within what is termed the 'spiritual' world as much as there is within the corridors of power. In the last century, the dark magi of the Psychopathic Control Grid have not only perfected their magic, but then destroyed it with over-use and rituals left half completed. In 1919, they had the magic of Wagner and Nietzsche to call upon. Today, they have descended into their metaphysical quagmire of trash magic, as they cast broken spells upon the human psyche with Lady Gaga and Justin Beiber.

Walpurgis Night is the story of the rise and fall of the aeon of Black-Häxan-Paganism, and how we, as a species, have survived the long night of the shadows thus far, and what this story tells us about the power of human decency in the face of the monsters. The course of history is a far stranger chart than any compass our 'captains' can provide us to navigate with.

Thomas Sheridan
Donard, County Wicklow, Ireland
March, 2014

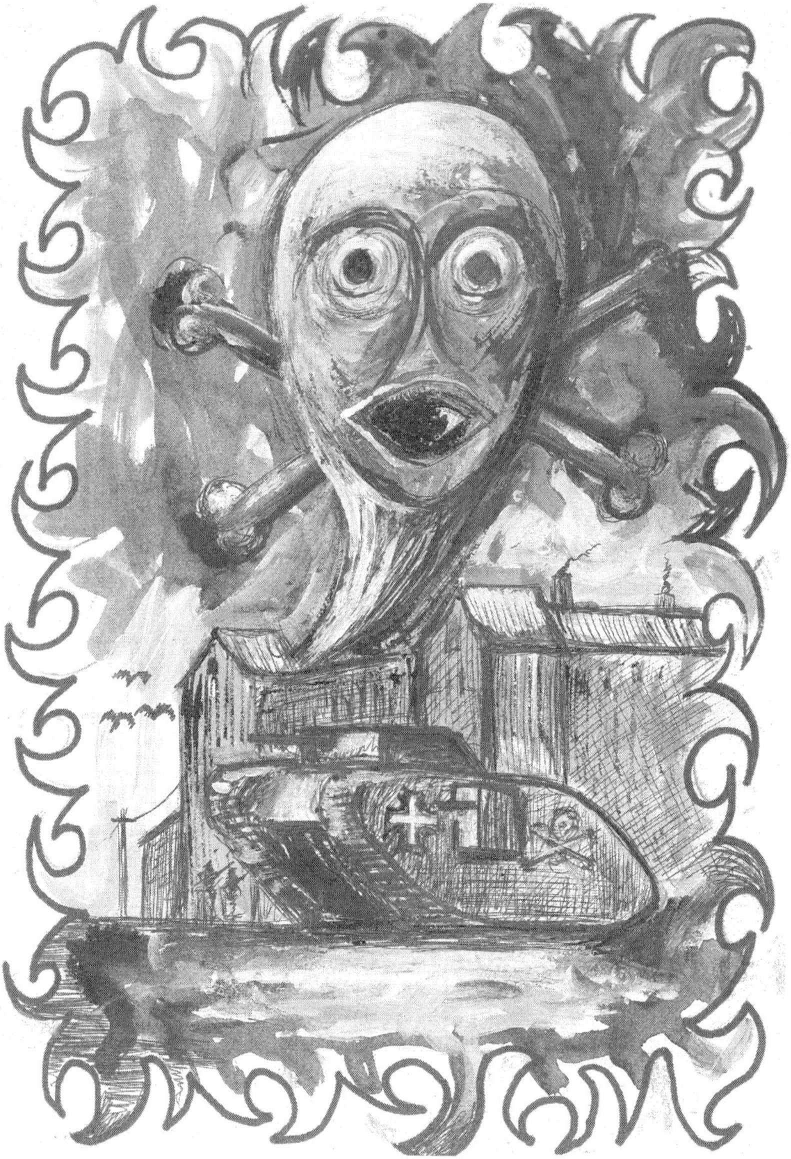

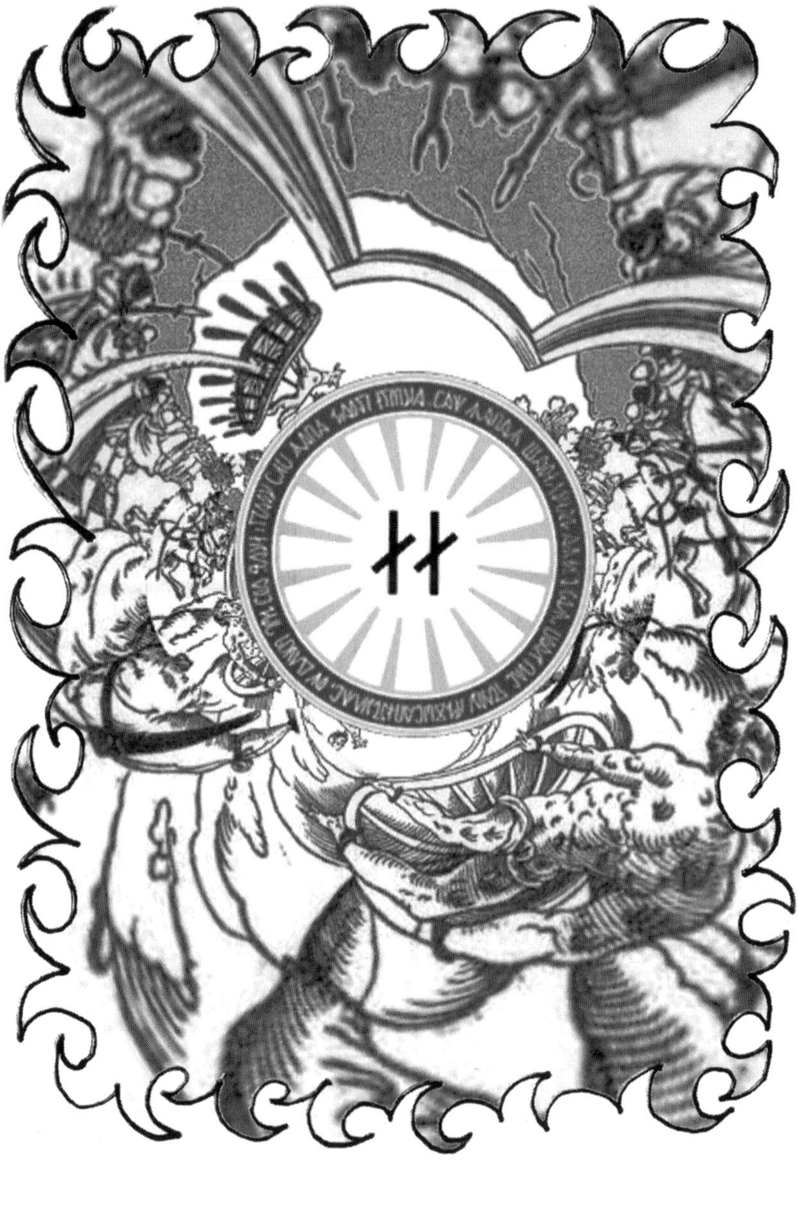

ONE

RUNES AMONG RUINS

"An appeal to fear never finds an echo in German hearts."
— Otto von Bismarck

When Red Army troops finally captured the Third Reich's Berlin bunker at the closing days of the Second World War, only to find (allegedly) the poorly-incinerated remains of both Adolf Hitler and his newly-wed wife Eva Braun in their shallow pit, most people—including the Allied leadership—were unaware that this was the culmination of an episode of history rooted in Hitler's Third Reich leadership, and to an extent, the German ruling class' pathological fascination with the occult, as well as Hitler's own psychopathic quest to control the perceptions of the people he targeted. It was borne of a desire to completely control the Germans' perceptions of both themselves and the world in general to such a level of profoundly terrifying devotion that it would cause an entire nation to become a kind of proto-psychopathic culture under the spell of the leader of the most powerful death cult the world has ever known.

Nationalism alone could not have made this happen. Another kind of force must have been called upon to reach such levels of apocalyptic mayhem. The gates of Hell had literally been opened in the years since 1919. These 'gates' remain open to the present day, and were not slammed shut with the Nuremberg hangings and suicides in 1946, as most would believe. The opening skirmishes which began in the human psyche during the latter decades of the 19th century and which raged within the material world all through the Great War, Bolshevik Revolutions, Second World War, Cold War and into the present-day War on Terror have never ceased. As I type these words, Russia and NATO are locked into a stalemate over the Ukraine, while the European Union follows much the same expansionist agenda as the Third Reich once did as it continually moves eastwards. The same magicians are still casting the same spells.

THE FATAL RECOIL

At the start of the British military involvement in the Second World War, one lone voice, the Scottish journalist Lewis Spence—who was also a folklorist and occult scholar—published a book in 1940 entitled *Occult Causes of the Present War*, in which he made it perfectly clear that the events which had taken place in Germany since the late Victorian era, and especially since the end of the Great War, were more than just a result of nationalism gone to the extreme. Spence was the first to promote the idea that there were very real 'demonic' influences behind Adolf Hitler and the Third Reich.

In *Occult Causes of the Present War*, Spence claimed that within the German psyche—just below the Christian conservative façade—there lies a repressed and deeply-entrenched hatred of Judeo-Christianity. Merging strands of Teutonic witchcraft with Luciferianism/Satanism (a kind of Black-Häxan-Paganism philosophy of might and power above all else), Spence essentially proposed that this Luciferianism/Satanism was the occult practice of the Prussian elite, and that (Häxan-Pagan) witchcraft was the true religion held within the rural Germanic mindscape, and then by earthly extension into that of the Third Reich's core values. Lewis Spence also proposed that the Third Reich had successfully managed to fuse these two ideas into a new form of demonic imperialism (which, for the purpose of the remainder of this book, I shall term Black-Häxan-Paganism).

He went on to state that the Nazi cult venerated the worship of the deities Odin (Wotan), Loki and Thor. The destructive nature of Loki was particularly appealing to the *SS* cult, as Fenrir, son of Loki, is predicted to break out of his prison to unleash the endtimes of *Ragnarök*, culminating in a huge battle, where the supernatural non-earthly forces, along with human beings and all the demons and nature spirits from the nine worlds, will fight in a cataclysmic battle.

This new Black-Häxan-Paganism state religion of Germany was further brought into consciousness by the proliferation of Teutonic secret societies which flourished in Germany until the rise of Hitler. Although Spence had a far more prosaic and personal understanding of the Nazi death cult, he was using overtly religious/Christian language (understandably so, as at the time, witchcraft was still a punishable offence in Britain) in order to attempt to get the message through to the British public as to what they were dealing with precisely. However, by then it was too late. Much too late.

During the publication of Spence's book in May 1940, the Battle of France between the British Expeditionary Force (BEF) and the German Blitzkrieg, a group of soldiers from the Royal Norfolk Regiment found themselves lost during the chaos, and were being pursued by the 14th Company, *SS Division Totenkopf*. The isolated British troops found themselves holding out in a rural farmhouse near the village of Le Paradis as *Waffen SS* forces descended on them. When the British troops ran out of ammunition, they surrendered to the *SS,* expecting to be treated as prisoners of war. Instead, they were marched to a barn, lined up alongside it and were machine gunned and casually stabbed, one by one, until the *SS* were satisfied that all 99 (2 survived) prisoners were dead. This was not just a war crime.

It was a ritualistic slaughter—based on the veneration and corruption of blood rites—which the *SS* were to perform everywhere from the shores of the Black Sea to the Atlantic and everywhere in between. Often, these atrocities involved the ritualistic burning alive of men, women and children inside churches, synagogues and other places of worship. Free French Forces that had escaped to Britain during the Dunkirk evacuation also told tales of the *Waffen SS* troops pulling down the crucifixes from every church they entered while proclaiming that Jesus Christ was "the bastard of the Jewish whore". Spence was proven correct. This was not a war against a military force alone, but a battle against a demonic cult of imperialist death and chaos.

THE CLOSING OF THE CIRCLE

On the night of the Teutonic Witches Sabbath, April 30, 1945, Hitler and his inner circle conducted the final death rites of a Black-Häxan-Paganism saga which began many years before, and had given birth to the greatest bloodbath the world has ever known. What began as a series of misconstrued psychedelic experiences by the young Adolf Hitler ended on *Walpurgisnacht* (Walpurgis Night): the night when witches take flight to the mountains and hold counsel with their demon gods. Right to the very end, Hitler maintained the theatrical sense of ritual which had brought him to power and gave him almost absolute stewardship of the Germanic consciousness for so long.

At the time of Hitler's remarkable rise to power and early military triumphs, many around the world marveled—as they still do to this very day—at Adolf Hitler's achievements, both impressive and horrifying. His often brilliant social, economic and industrial reforms, along with his uncanny, and at times, almost supernatural intuition as a military strategist still remain awesome and terrifying in their magnitude, ambition and inhumanity. So much so, that most observers in the immediate aftermath of the Second World War were unable to comprehend the incredible psychological hold which Hitler and National Socialism held over the German people.

Why, even after his death, were so many Germans still willing to fight on and die for the man who brought their nation to complete and total ruin? Many of the most fanatical *SS* troops who fought in Berlin to the last bullet were not even Germans. Numerous academics and ordinary people had asked themselves time and time again: how could Hitler accumulate such remarkable devotion and power? Their speculation concerning the rise of Hitler was due to most people having almost no understanding that both Adolf Hitler and several of his henchmen were highly skilled sorcerers (and this is not hyperbole) who very literally spellbound—firstly, the Germans and then the entire human race—and that the spells they cast back then are still transforming the reality of the planet right to the very present.

Adolf Hitler was a master of mind control as well as having a hypnotic—many believed 'demonic'—ability to unleash fanatical devotion in others, and this ability to keep people enchanted by his persona was, at his very essence, the stock and trade of his Black-Häxan-Pagan occultism. Not only was he the leader of Germany; he was Germany and Germany was Hitler, and his Third Reich was—in very real terms—a Black-Häxan-Paganism empire under his absolute rule and total psychopathic control. In 1942, Hitler stated, "My whole life can be summed up as this ceaseless effort of mine to persuade other people." He wasn't speaking in metaphor.

How did Hitler—an otherwise very average small town man—develop such powers of persuasion, and how central was his interest, if not devotion, to the occult, integral to his remarkable ability to captivate an entire nation who then followed him into their eventual abyss which millions of Germans and other nationalities gave to Hitler and the Third Reich so willingly, and often with a level of mass hysteria and blood thirsty fanaticism unequalled in history before or since?

In many cases, the devotion they demonstrated to the Third Reich only returned back upon them, as the 20th *Waffen Grenadier Division of the SS* (1st Estonian) were to discover during their 'Czech Hell', along with the almost complete annihilation of the *Feldhernhalle* Panzergrenadier Division during the Siege of Budapest, who also found out that there was quite literally Hell to pay when there was nowhere left to run, and no Third Reich left to return to. Unconditional service to their Führer often came with a horrific price. If you were a top-ranking Nazi war criminal, your chances of surviving the war—via being 'spirited' away by the almost mythical ODESSA (*Organisation der ehemaligen SS*)—and living out the rest of your life in luxury, were far higher than that of the average German civilian or military man. As we shall see in future volumes of this series of books, the Second World War did not end in 1945; it was more a case of a new form of geo-political hypnosis being unleashed upon the human psyche.

In this series, I will be utilising my knowledge of how psychopathology functions within control structures, via social engineering, occult sciences, cults, behaviourism and especially the arts. I will also attempt to make it clear that pathological leadership and the dark occult sciences were, and continue to be, one and the same thing; and that Adolf Hitler was the first in a line of modern witch kings at the centre of his purposefully created maelstrom of Black-Häxan-Paganism and ritual sacrifice. In this first book, I hope to present the most comprehensive understanding of the occult nature of Germany between the end of the Great War and Adolf Hitler's rise to power in 1933, which will be free from any personal religious/political prejudices, historical axe-grinding, tabloid style sensationalism and other superficial moral platitudes just for the sake of it. We know that Hitler and the Third Reich were evil.

MAGIC AND MIND CONTROL

When I use the term 'magic', I am not referring exclusively to clandestine occult rituals or spells, incantations and ceremonies alone, for the issue goes far deeper than these obvious stereotypes. The art and science of causing change in the material world is profoundly complex, broad-ranging and more prevalent in our world than most people are aware of. It also encompasses the use of words, symbolism, the performing arts, education, propaganda, psychology, human sexuality and even popular entertainment. The Third Reich was the first society to so completely merge the magic of ritual with the magic of the spotlight so perfectly into a consciousness-bombarding totality. The Entertainment-Military-Industrial Complex was a Nazi invention, and you are still under its spell.

WHAT IS MAGIC?

The most commonly accepted definition of the term magic is: 'the application of Science and Art in conformity with will in order to create change within the material world'. Keep these terms in mind for the remainder of this book: *science, art, change* and *will*. These are the basic concepts behind what we have come to know as magic. Spells, candlelight rituals, fire, incantations, sigils, charms and other trappings of the sorcerer's trade are purely optional. Ritual or ceremonial magic, as we shall discuss later on in this book, in the Nordic world would have been known as Häxan (Witches) or Teutonic or Pagan Revival Magic. Adolf Hitler and the inner core of the Third Reich utilised all of these methods to gain control of, and then to manipulate millions of people into conformity with the will of National Socialism. The book of spell craft written to indoctrinate the German consciousness into accepting this new spiritual path was Adolf Hitler's own autobiography, *Mein Kampf*, enchanting (in the occult sense) Hitler's rituals into essentially a Satanic manifesto philosophically fusing with social-Darwinism/socio-political ideology (art and science) themes into a 'might is right' spell for the collectively broken and lost Teutonic soul.

A magic spell can be simply a manifesto, blueprint or satire designed to create a change in the opinions and psychology of those who read it or are exposed to it. Magic, as a means of change, is rooted in Natural Philosophy, which is how science was generally known before the *Enlightenment*. The scientific aspect of magic is likewise crucial for the reader to grasp at this point, as it will become very apparent when topics such as *Darwinism, Eugenics* and *Racial Hygiene* towards creating a Master Race are discussed later in this book.

As uncomfortable as this makes the average atheist, Heinrich Himmler—the occult-obsessed *Reichsführer* of the *Schutzstaffel (SS)* —and his attempted creation of an *Aryan Master Race* was a deeply scientific pursuit in the overall concept of magic. They are simply one and same thing, as the Nazis had reverted the cultural clock of scientific methodology back to a pre-*Enlightenment* version of what science was considered to be prior to Descartes, and closer to that of Natural Philosophy and alchemy. Hence, why they may have enjoyed a huge technical advantage for so long compared to the rest of the world at that time (with the exception of radar and tank design) which never really caught up with the technical and engineering capabilities of the Third Reich.

Nazi scientists were operating within an almost alchemical methodology (along with unlimited slave labour and disregard for human rights), and were morally unbounded when it came to research and development while working within an occult culture where *High Strangeness* became the norm. Take, for instance, the highly unusual aircraft, the Blohm & Voss BV 141, with its asymmetrical, single-engine and cockpit mounted on the main wing, which was developed and placed into production in 1940. The appearance of the aircraft, even today, is visually so surreal that it presents an excellent insight into how engineering and scientific development within the Third Reich was operating by their own rules, unlike anywhere else in the world at the time. The reason for this was that their sense of self and entire cognitive processing was functioning towards a 'magical' end, rather than an exclusively materialist one alone.

Magic is referred to as a science, in that there are specific steps and procedures which must be undertaken in order to create change in conformity with will. Magic is also referred to as an art, in that some people are more talented at magic than others, in precisely the same way some people are more talented at playing the violin than others. Think of a page of sheet music; that would be the *SCIENCE*. The interpretation of the sheet music by the violinist would be the *ART*, and the *CHANGE* would be the emotional and psychological effect a performance of the music would have upon the person or people listening to the concert. Magic can also be the creation of a material object which was previously nonexistent in the material world. Another example would be an architect designing a building on a sheet of paper or an AutoCad PC program, and from this, the house, office block or bridge is then created. The structural and engineering expertise of the architect's design is the *SCIENCE*, the beauty and usefulness of the structure is the *ART*, and the *CHANGE* is all the new possibilities this new building unleashes. This is also magic in the truest definition of the word.

MAGIC IN THE SUBCONSCIOUS WORLD

However, if a magician is possessed with a tenacity and a powerful intent—to specifically target the deep subconscious layers of the mind, both in the personal and collective sense—then the very fabric of reality can be altered. New paradigms and environments can be literally constructed in real time and at an incredible social pace by offering up panaceas of utopias and unfulfilled fantasies. Entirely new versions of reality can be brought into the material world which were first created as (provisionally imposed) ideas in the minds of willing targets. This is the most powerful form of sorcery of all: the conformity of the will of others with that of the will of the magician(s).

HITLER AND THE CRAFT

It has also been noted by many academics that there was never any hard proof that Hitler ever personally took part in, or conducted magical rituals. However, the same academics also note that there is no actual document signed by Hitler in which he ordered the *Final Solution* either. These academics proceed to use anecdotal and other (highly conclusive) evidence to show that although there is no specific historical documentation to prove that Adolf Hitler ordered and knew about the Holocaust, when all is said and done, and when one looks objectively at the full picture, the overwhelming evidence is there: that Hitler did know and he did 'order' it. Hitler was a cunning magician and wordsmith, knowing that for change to be brought about in others, the *anvil of the psyche* within the minds of men must first be constructed through association and subliminal suggestion. In the course of this book, I will apply the same methodology towards the issue of Hitler and the occult sciences. I believe there is more than ample evidence to suggest that Hitler (and his Third Reich leadership) was aware of 'the craft', and his understanding of ritual and ceremony indicates he took part in magical practices, from divination to sex magic.

To further illustrate that he was no stranger to occult circles, it is documented that when Adolf Hitler came to power, he wasn't long in office before he offered to fly the British artist and well-known occultist Austin Osman Spare to Berlin to paint the Führer's portrait. Austin Osman Spare had come to Hitler's attention as Spare had previously painted a self-portrait entitled *Self as Hitler*, which was a hybrid of Spare and Adolf Hitler, leaving no doubt that he was aware of Hitler's own occult status beyond that of politician. The painting eventually, in time, came into the ownership of famous British journalist and occultist Hannen Swaffer.

Along with being surrounded by occultists, for most of his adult life, while also being submerged within a culture where membership of occult societies was hardly an obscure pursuit (400,000 German troops in the Great War of 1914-18 were members of occult groups), it is also worth noting that among Hitler's own personal library of over seven thousand books—which were discovered in an abandoned salt mine near Berchtesgaden by the US 101st Airborne Division in 1945—contained several occult and esoteric works which were at the time, and still continue to be brushed aside as mere 'Nazi Tripe'. Hitler was an avid and studious reader. The careful notes he left inside these books—now practically hidden in the *Third Reich Collection* within the US Library of Congress—attest to this. Among this 'tripe' is a deeply significant volume with a dedication on the fly leaf which reads 'To Adolf Hitler, my dear brother in Armanen'. What makes this so significant is that the term 'Armanen' (Teutonic

Magicians) was used exclusively by occultist Guido von List—perhaps the most influential European occult revivalist of the 19th century—and is clearly dedicated to his 'brother' Adolf Hitler. This is nothing less than one cult member addressing another.

Adolf Hitler was also registered with three public libraries in Linz, and during his time in Vienna—prior to the Great War of 1914-18—he practically lived the Hofbibliothek, the former court library of the Hapsburgs, which contained many of the esoteric and alchemical texts formerly belonging to the Holy Roman Emperor, Rudolf II of Bohemia. Yet all of this is brushed aside by academic historians, when the reality remains that Adolf Hitler had—during his formative years—access to some of the most comprehensive collections of occult science and magical books in the world.

August Kubizek, Hitler's friend during the years in Vienna, wrote, "I just can't imagine Adolf without books. He had them piled up around him at home. He always had a book with him wherever he went. Books were his world." This dismissal of Hitler's scholarship potential stands alongside the other 'given' that Hitler was a poor painter of little talent. This *de rigueur* nonsense is still offered up as proof of some kind of moral academic credentials within the mainstream. The fact is that Hitler was both well-read and a skilled painter. Accepting these realities is important in order to understand what drove him psychologically and emotionally.

Another factor for lack of evidence of esoteric and occult involvement during his early life is due to Hitler having had much of his personal history during his formative 'occult' years scrubbed from the records after he rose to power. Although he was only listed as a 'guest' of the very powerful occult Thule Society in Munich, this was not unusual, as he was still in the army at the time, and membership of secret organisations was frowned upon by the Bavarian military. As a result, most army men in the Thule Combat League and Society had their membership status listed as 'guest'.

Long after he came to power, Hitler's speeches were still filled with the phrasing and symbolism of Armanism and Ariosophy—the Teutonic variants of Theosophy—on which the Thule Society based much of their ideals and occult rituals. Herman Rauchning, the leader of the Nazi enclave of Danzig, noted a conversation he had with Adolf Hitler, during a private event after he became Führer, which leaves no doubt that Hitler was a serious—if highly secretive—occultist, with far more knowledge of the 'art' than he ever publicly stated.

Rauchning, paraphrasing Hitler, stated, "To have 'magical insight' was apparently Hitler's idea of a goal of human progress. He himself felt that he already had the rudiments of the gift. He attributed to it his success and future eminence. A savant of Munich...had also written some curious stuff about the prehistoric world, about myths. And visions of early man, about forms of perceptions and supernatural powers. There was the eye of Cyclops, or median eye, the organ of magic perception of the Infinite, now reduced to a rudimentary pineal gland. Speculations of this sort fascinated Hitler and he would sometimes be entirely wrapped up upon them. He saw his own remarkable career as a confirmation of hidden powers. He saw himself as chosen for superhuman tasks, as the prophet of the rebirth of man in a new form."

Notice the psychopathic, cult leader megalomania in Hitler's understanding of his own place in history. When psychopathic personality meets occult knowledge, and then meets power, the unleashing of a monstrous catastrophe(s) can be the only outcome. Which is why ancient societies and the *Mysteries Schools* from the Gnostics to the pre-Bavarian Illuminati and on to the Golden Dawn were always very strict about whom they allowed to become a member, and once inside, there were specific tests and levels of indoctrination which had to be overcome constantly, in order to root out the self-serving adepts.

In Germany, between the Franco-Prussian War and the Great War of 1914-18, there existed an occult free-for-all, where the secrets and rituals of the magicians were easily obtained from magazines such as *Ostara*, only to eventually fall into the hands of a young Adolf Hitler, who was an avid reader of the publication, and who went to the trouble of acquiring the full collection of published editions. In *Ostara*, Hitler would have been exposed to magical practices and techniques such as night rituals, blood magic, fascination (eye magic) and 'electrical' sex magic, all of which Hitler was to employ in order to attain power over both people and nations.

THE BOOK IN THE WINDOW

In 1912, an Austrian economist by the name of Dr. Walter Stein, who was also an acclaimed scholar of Byzantine art, procured a second-hand copy of *Parsifal* from an occult bookstore in Vienna. *Parsifal* is a thirteenth-century Grail Romance concerning the original chalice which Jesus and the Twelve Disciples were alleged to have used, during the initial *Transubstantiation* of the blood of Christ, and this ritual still remains central to the Catholic mass to this day. Keenly interested in the history of the Middle Ages, Dr. Stein would have been aware of the numerous locations around Europe where the Holy Grail and other sacred relics were purported to be held.

However, there was one item that interested Dr. Stein above all else. That was the Holy Lance, or as Hitler and the Third Reich referred to it decades later: *Heilige Lanze* or 'The Spear of Destiny'. The ultimate Wonder Weapon. Synchronistically, as is common with major turning points in human history, it was the small matter of the margin notes pencilled in by the previous owner of *Parsifal* that was to change the course of human history. It is mainly composed as brief notes on Germanic, Norse and Slavic mythology, along with what was to become known later as *Racial Magic,* which is the belief that certain races have superhuman or occult powers (a commonly held, if not politically incorrect belief worldwide) contained within their blood, and, in the case of this edition of *Parsifal*, Germanic or Teutonic Racial Magic. Returning later to the second-hand bookshop, Dr. Stein asked the shop owner if he was aware of the previous owner of the book who made the notes in the margins. The shop owner did know who this was: a young, semi-professional street artist named Adolf Hitler.

Upon meeting Hitler, Dr. Stein was amazed and fascinated by the young man's complex knowledge of the legends of the Middle Ages and, in particular, Teutonic and Norse mythology. However, of all the things which Hitler spoke about with messianic zeal, one more than any other—The Spear of Destiny—was what Dr. Stein recalled the young artist being almost completely consumed by. Having observed the Holy Lance first-hand at the Hofburg Museum in Vienna, Adolf Hitler, like so many, came to believe that it truly was the actual weapon used by a Roman Centurion that pierced the side of Jesus Christ as he lay dying on the cross during an act of compassion. Legend then has it that the young Roman soldier had himself what we would now consider a 'psychedelic' experience, in which he came to realise that he had pierced the side of God Himself. At this point, the Heilige Lanze, or The Spear of Destiny, became the ultimate magical wand, and, if in the hands of the most powerful magician, would become the ultimate 'Wonder Weapon'.

Hitler told Dr. Stein about the psychedelic experience he'd had inside the museum in Vienna when he first laid eyes on the spear. "I slowly became aware of a mighty presence around it. I sensed a great destiny awaited me and I knew beyond contradiction that the blood in my veins would one day become the Folk Spirit of My people." Later, this would be encapsulated in that hypnotic and now notorious mantra: 'Ein Volk. Ein Reich." It would take another quarter of a century before Adolf Hitler would become the greatest Black-Häxan-Paganism sorcerer of the 20th century, and hold in his possession the wonder weapon he so longed to acquire, and which may have eventually possessed him and his fellow countrymen, with terrifying results.

Aside from the fact that there are two other pointed blades in existence also claiming the titles of the Holy Lance—one being in Paris and the other in the Vatican—this one in particular was the one known as the 'Hapsburgs Lance', which belonged to the Royal Hapsburgs dynasty that enjoyed a most remarkable historical and supernatual legacy. Ownership of these supreme magical relics being in the hands of elite bloodlines is not at all unusual. For example, the Shroud of Turin will not be subject to examination unless tribute is first paid to the Italian aristocratic family who owns the relic. People unaware of how magic actually functions may be forgiven for considering it absurd that there were three Holy Lances in existence in Europe which were probably all fakes. Hence, how could the Hapsburgs Lance in the Hofburg Museum in Vienna have any more 'powers' than the others?

According to the occult, the very act of ascribing a 'magical' history, experience or legend upon a relic will infuse that object with tremendous 'psychic energy'. Multiply this by several centuries, rumours, legends and sincere adoration, and the object—even if it began life as a crude forgery inside an obscure blacksmith's workshop—with the psychic energy poured into it by the 'true believers' can be literally 'charged' with all the energy required for it to become a magical facsimile of the object it claims to be. If enough human concentration, applied mythology and even a sense of dread and foreboding (think of the Ark of the Convenant for example) is focused on the object over many centuries, then it essentially becomes what it is proclaimed to be.

The Hapsburgs lance that Hitler was entranced by appears to have its origin in Antioch (a ruined city now located in modern-day Turkey, and which was once an important city on the Old Silk Road leading from the Orient). During the Crusades, the Holy Lance was located there while the city was under siege by the Saracens. Eventually, the lance was liberated and returned to Austria—via an impressive 'who's who' of Germanic history—and then fell into the hands of the soon-to-be incredibly powerful Hapsburgs Dynasty, which, until 1918, ruled over an enormous empire across central and south eastern Europe with bloodline infiltration into the royal families of Spain and France.

According to the Teutonic mythology which so captivated Hitler all his life, this lance was the 'wonder weapon' carried by the Christian emperor Charlemagne, and was used to win 47 decisive victories over his enemies. With each successive military victory, the legend of the Holy Lance of Antioch grew to spellbound all who spoke of it, and it came to furnish Charlemagne with the reputation of being one of the giants of pre-Renaissance European history.

The magic and power of the lance only increased in intensity when Charlemagne died instantly upon letting it fall from his grasp. Following Charlemagne, the Holy Lance became the wonder weapon of the Saxon king Heinrich during his successful military campaign against Poland. It was then passed down into the hands of another giant of European history, Frederick Barbarossa, who was to plunder the Italian peninsula, eventually driving the Pope out of Rome, and ostensibly putting an end to the claims that the Vatican had the real Holy Lance. Eventually, it would become the personal possession of Adolf Hitler, who had the relic held in a special shrine in Nuremberg, the high altar of Nazi mass rituals.

THE MAGUS UNFOLDS

Do all these factors and associations conclusively prove that Adolf Hitler personally took part and conducted occult magical rituals? Not necessarily, but we cannot rule out the possibility either, as the results are self-evident in terms of his power over people and the circles he moved in. I speculate too that Hitler may have gone through a stage of initiation rites within occult sciences before he became politically active, and then came to realise that all magical ritual is undertaken towards concentrating the will of the magician into a powerful dynamic force. Once the will of the magician is developed to a required level of energetic forcefulness, no further occult magic rituals are needed. Think of it in the same terms as a college student getting their degree and then going off to work in their chosen profession. The days of intensive study are behind them. They are now adepts utilising their schooling in the real world. This issue of Hitler's hypnotic power over so many people has been a burning question among academic historians and lay people alike since the Second World War ended. As early as 1946, and well into 1947—when millions of Germans still remained faithful to Hitler's 'struggle'—writers such as Hugh Trevor-Roper in his book *The Last Days of Hitler* attempted to rationalise this surreal period of history by portraying Hitler in sweeping epic terms as possessing a quality beyond ordinary human capabilities. For this, Trevor-Roper was to receive a death threat from the notorious Stern Gang, a group of Jewish ex-Nazi hunters who were wary of a less than prosaic concept of Hitler—other than the murderous genocidal dictator—taking root within the population as a whole. So concerned were people in the immediate aftermath of the war, that Hitler—even in death—might achieve a kind of epic status in the consciousness of outside observers, that an understandable agreement of self-censorship was the unspoken rule when discussing the more esoteric aspects of the Third Reich.

Returning Allied troops also spoke of the fanaticism and almost robotic nature of the *SS* and the Hitler Youth they encountered, unable to comprehend how a Charlie Chaplin look-a-like could procure such self-destructive devotion from these young men who threw away their lives for their Führer, even when it was a completely pointless act of sacrifice. These returning soldiers brought back daggers, flags, regalia and other Nazi artefacts from the European war inscribed with strange designs and insignia: the magical symbols of the *Waffen SS*. The psychological impact of all this was almost too much for people outside Germany to deal with.

I suspect that this subconscious fear of the occult-brainwashed German soldier—untroubled by death—resulted in a kind of cultural compensatory archetype via their portrayal as buffoon-like half-wits in television shows ranging from the American series *Hogan's Heroes*, to the BBC's 1980's sitcom *'Allo 'Allo!* Such images prevented people from having to confront the terrifying actual reality of the *Waffen SS*, or the vicious cruelty and sadistic efficiency of the *Gestapo*.

Furthermore, there was something different about Germany under the Third Reich that made it so very strange and alien to other countries and cultures at the time. This sense of Nazi-era Germanic otherworldliness existing outside the accepted moral parameters only increased as the details of the Nazi death camps and other atrocities filtered through into world media. Authors such as Lewis Spence and

Hugh Trevor-Roper had correctly identified that Adolf Hitler had a wizard-like ability to call forth the repressed Teutonic supernatural archetypes which lurked in the dark woodlands, marshes and foreboding mountain passes of the collective Germanic psyche, and that by using the weaponised magical rituals of the Third Reich, these pre-Christian gods of war, power and death were there to be resurrected.

This is an analysis also presented by Carl Jung, and one I fully concur with and one which will be revealed in stark clarity as we look deeper into this topic. Hitler and his Nazi Party had the German people spellbound in a very literal sense and, on some level, most people—especially academics—went into a kind of collective denial that such a thing could ever have happened in the past, for fear that is could somehow happen again and in another country.

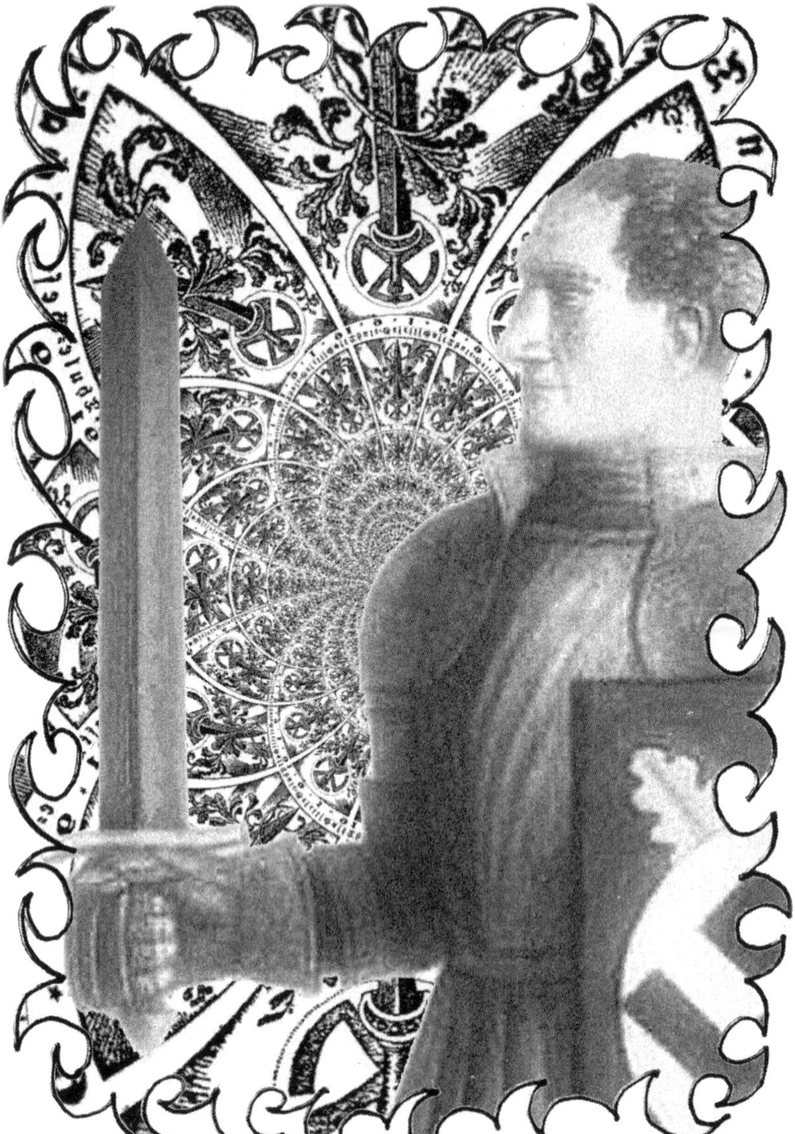

TWO

THE TEMPLES OF THE MIND

"That there is a Devil, is a thing doubted by none but such as are under the influences of the Devil."

— Cotton Mather

While historians embarked on enormous and complex histories of the rise and fall of Hitler and the Third Reich, what they failed to include within these works speaks volumes, as the Thule Society is hardly mentioned at all, if ever. This would be akin to a history of Christianity without mentioning, or playing down the importance of the Old Testament. I have no doubt that these historians knew full well that Adolf Hitler and the Nazis were an occult magical order first and foremost, and by ignoring this Nazi 'tripe' they could scrub it from the realities of the period. Their 'rational' academic minds self-censored the notion that political, social and historical leadership structures of huge power and influence could, in any way, be connected with the supernatural. By doing so, they might also be forced to look at all political systems since the end of the Second World War, and contend with the terrifying realisation that among world leaders, within the media and big business, and continuing right to the very present, the monster of magic and occult forces might actually be under the bed after all. They are wrong, of course, in their culture of denial in regards to Nazis and the occult. As long as psychopaths continue to hold sway at the top of our national power structure, it only takes one charismatic leader with the same magical insights and know-how as Adolf Hitler had to cast the same spells that he did between 1919 and 1945.

It has been happening non-stop ever since. Tragically for the human race as a whole, certain elements within the Allied powers were so impressed with the achievements and abilities of the Third Reich, that in the years 1946 and 1947, they rebranded much of the black arts of the Nazis and exported them beyond the ruins of post-war Germany. Weapons which once terrified Europe—adorned with the insignia of the swastika on them—were later adorned with that of the US and USSR's five pointed pentagram: another magical symbol. It wasn't just the weapons of the battlefield that the Allied Powers captured from the Nazis and perfected for their own ends. The weapons of the human psyche being used against itself also found a new home outside the ruins of the Third Reich.

THE UNSPOKEN SECRET

Adolf Hitler achieved all he did between 1919 and 1945 with little more than a basic state school education. But he did, however, possess an uncanny charisma which gave him the ability to not only get inside the mind of the target(s), but to also offer the target(s) the panaceas to repair the missing ghosts in their soul. Germany, following the Versailles Treaty, was a land of endless ghosts, cripples and broken, fractured consciousness which needed more than just a repair. They needed a Teutonic messiah. Hitler was first and foremost a Black-Häxan-Paganism practitioner, and thus gave them a dark Christ of chaos, offering redemption for the Germanic soul. Hitler was indeed very charismatic in the eyes of many, but the term does not necessarily imply likability, decency and kindness. The Devil, for example, is often described as charismatic. Charisma has its etymology in the Greek language and indicates 'divine grace' or 'bestowed gifts'. The term does not denote—in its original meaning—great altruistic attributes. It simply states that the individual has powers from beyond this earthly realm. However, these powers can be both good and bad. Charisma is very much a neutral term. It all depends on which side is bestowing the power to the mortal who invokes it.

There had already been a cultural need for charismatic leadership ingrained within German intellectual circles following the work of the social theorist Max Weber, whose insights on the condition were very influential in the late Victorian era. Weber stated that for a German politician to be possessed with the gift of charismatic leadership, he must also carry with him a powerful sense of conviction similar to that of a religious fundamentalist. Weber went on to theorise that the Germanic people, from their cultural and imperial conditioning, were looking for more than just a 'bread and butter' issues political leader, but one who would take them on a kind of mystical quest beyond the trappings of day-to-day political necessities. The Germanic temperament at the time Hitler rose to power craved a godly-king at the helm of their ship of state, and not just an administrative bureaucracy to replace the failing Weimar Republic set up in the wake of the Versailles Treaty. Hitler's public and political manifestation—in combination with the engineered collapse of the Weimar Republic—could not have fit the bill more perfectly.

It was almost as if he had been 'divinely' created to be the perfect leader of Germany when the population needed their messiah the most. A Teutonic warrior king with supernatural abilities to lead them on a quest for the restoration of their individual and social honour, as well as to keep inflation in check and deal with ingrained cultural insecurities, arrogance and grievances. The Germans got more than a saviour brandishing a swastika and leading their nation to honour and glory. They also got a witch king leading them into their eventual inferno.

When one looks at Hitler on video today, we are often struck by how unremarkable he seems. An almost absurd character waving his arms about, sporting a silly moustache along with a schoolboy's haircut. But what we are looking at is the material Adolf Hitler. This is not what the German people of the time beheld when they looked at the leader of National Socialism. Instead, their desires and inclinations extruded the supernatural Hitler from below the surface which was more akin to a furious cauldron of glorious ideals than that of the mere mortal man on the surface delivering them. There was one other aspect which does not come across in these newsreels and photos: Hitler's eyes, and in particular, his stare. The piercing gaze which could mesmerise both schoolboy and British Prime Ministers alike. That was the Hitler that captured the collective Germanic mind, heart and soul. That stare was the shadow of the Black-Häxan-Paganism behind the curtain.

THE WILL TO CONQUEST

Hitler's fascination with the occult and magic—which he carried to his final moments (if official Russian Soviet and US accounts are to be believed)—while he held out deep inside a dank and chaotic Berlin bunker as Red Army shells rained down upon the ruins of his empire, was the end of a life story rooted in the mystical, the magical and the esoteric. A story which was and is still also deeply rooted within Teutonic cultural and folk traditions, as well as ethnic folk superstitions of the supernatural and magic.

More than any other aspect of his craft, Hitler, like any true magician, understood that by tapping into the deeply held and repressed neuroses, dreams, ideals and, most importantly of all, the subconscious fears of the Germanic peoples, he could unleash within them an almost supernatural devotion to him. Hitler successfully unleashed these traits and much, much more. However, the story of Hitler and the occult is ultimately one of catastrophic failure; the repercussions of which remain with us to this day. This is the message we must garnish from this tale of the swastika and the sorcerer: that 'magic'—in its absolute and most practical form—can offer both salvation and annihilation. In what was the savage irony of having set about proclaiming to liberate Germany from its humiliation and suffering, the German people eventually endured the greatest humiliation and suffering of all.

Hitler's rise and fall is a powerful and sobering example of what happens when magic fails, or more accurately, when the 'demons' inside the mind of man replace that of the man himself, and from this, spread like an infection to targeted minds, excavated by their own needs and neuroses, which then spreads even further, like a demonic hellfire, engulfing all it touches.

A RITUAL LEFT INCOMPLETE

Yet there can be no denying that for at least a decade or more, the magical spells and sorcery of Adolf Hitler and the Third Reich were a spectacular success in terms of the objectives of National Socialism, along with effectively addressing the demands and objectives of Germany's domestic and foreign policy, which left the world looking on in paralysing awe. So much so, that the elite of the world (and particularly those of the Anglo-American stock) were left wondering how they could get a piece of the action for themselves.

Visiting American athletes had to do all they could to restrain themselves and *not* make a 'Seig Heil' salute during the opening ceremony of the *1936 Berlin Olympics*, as they found themselves caught in a melatonin-saturated magic spell beyond even that which the bright lights of their own beloved Broadway could offer. Adolf Hitler, tapping into the deepest aspect of the Germanic psyche, coupled with his deep understanding of Germanic mythology, as well as capitalising on his own knowledge of the occult, did precisely that. Let us reconsider the title of the well-known 1935 film created by movie director and propagandist Leni Riefenstahl, entitled, *Triumph of the Will* in the context of the term 'Will', being very much part and parcel of magical theory, and a picture begins to emerge of something much more than that of a man who rose to power to lead an empire and then started the Second World War. This lack of understanding of Hitler's true motivations and full extent of the effects of his occult psychological manipulation abilities is the main reason why mainstream academics fail to fully comprehend this era of history. They can debate, analyse, research and trawl through the minutiae of social, economic, political and economic history of Adolf Hitler and the Third Reich; but however, without the understanding of the occult and application of the magic used upon the German people and eventually, the entire world, these historians are missing the one key aspect of how these spectacular and terrifying changes manifested outwardly from central Europe between 1919 and 1945, only to contract again into its still mysterious and cataclysmic "terminal event", as Albert Speer, the Nazi armaments minister, described the defeat of the German war machine.

THE MAGI, THE MIND, THE TIME AND THE PLACE

When one thinks of the Germans, a deep collective superstition of magic and the supernatural is hardly the first thing that springs to mind. Such imagery does not sit well with the stereotypes of the modern, efficient German on the forefront of science and industry creating modern technology within a technical environment sterilised free from irrationality and superstition. The Germanic races have been around for a very long time, and the modern version of the technical, no-nonsense German is a relatively new one. It arose primarily as a result of two factors: the *Prussian Education Model* in the years leading up to a spectacular victory over France in the Franco-Prussian War (1870-71) and the necessities of the Industrial Revolution, and, in particular, the move away from guilds and towards apprenticeships. The stereotypical German we think of today is a direct result of these social and cultural changes within Germany during the mid- to late-Victorian era. However, there is a very deep well of subconscious layers to the Germanic psyche which never went away completely.

THOR AND THE OAK MEN

What makes Teutonic magic and occult folklore so interesting compared to other canons of European rites is firstly, its powerful connection to the forests and woodlands, and secondly, the darkness and physical brutality of the rites and rituals which have been recorded over the centuries by Grimm and other Germanic folklorists. In his book, *The Settlement and Colonisation of Europe*,

Richard Koebner stated that among the pre-Christian Germans, 'the heart of the forest was the seat of the Godhead: there its awe; there it claimed its sacrifice and humble submission...'

In the year 98 AD, Tacticus wrote that at certain times of the year, all Teutonic tribes of the same blood would gather at a certain forest that their delegations considered to be hallowed by visions beheld by their ancestors. Until late into the Christian era, Germans would celebrate *Weihnachtstage*, the consecrated nights during the *Winter Solstice*. They buried their dead with their heads pointing to the East in anticipation of the rebirth of Ostara. As late as the 19th century German priests were still incorporating forests and, in particular, the oak, into their Christian ceremonies. The temples of the Teutonic wizards were the old woods, and this later became the towering columns of the Gothic cathedrals. In 1724, historian Bishop Warburton noted that Gothic architecture was 'ingeniously projected' to resemble sacred Germanic groves as a direct emotional and psychological link to their ancestors of the Teutonic forest tribes and religions of Germany. The worship of the oak—both the leaves and acorns—inside the grove by the Teutonic Häxan priests who conducted their rituals inside these groves by flaming torchlight, is precisely the same manner the National Socialists would perform their own torchlight rituals under towering Nazi banners. The great rallies of Nuremberg and other Nazi grand affairs were nothing more than the Häxan priestly rituals of the groves brought up to date. The oak was also the symbol of construction, rebuilding and restoration, both materially and spiritually. This led to the *Reichsarbeitsdienst* (Reich Labour Service) created by the Nazis, who used the symbol of a spade stylised to look like an acorn adorned on either side by oak leaves on their flag along with other regalia. The depth and significance of the oak symbolism being updated by the National Socialist party cannot be understated, as its restoration also unleashed dark archetypal undercurrents of the Teutonic psyche which had been repressed for centuries by a shim of Christianity. The sacredness of the oak in Teutonic Häxan magic is recalled in J.G. Frazer's epic work on magical ritual, *The Golden Bough*, in which he outlines the serious consequences of stripping the bark from an oak tree. The culprit's navel would be nailed to the area of the oak where the bark had been stripped and then they would be forced to walk around the tree trunk until their intestines had become completely unraveled—as a sort of bandage—around the area of stripped oak bark. Then the guilty person would die, and from this, nourishing the roots of the oak with the life force of their blood. The life of a man for the life of an oak.

The task of protection of the oaks was given to young men in the service of the Teutonic wizard—a Häxan variation of the Catholic altar boy—referred to as 'Oak Men'. Their service was to Donar or

Thunar, both being alternate names for the Norse deity Thor. Donar, who was also the Italian pagan god Jupiter, was connected with fertility, spring rains and the end of the darkness of winter. The Teutonic traditions of the Yule Log and the Easter Oak all derive from the Donar/Oak cult of the survival of Winter and the oncoming revival and restoration of Spring.

During the era of National Socialism, the young men of the *Reichsarbeitsdienst* would perform large-scale rituals based around the assumption that their labour and tools were performing this same task. Their spades were planting new groves for the Nazi wizard class to perform their own rituals, and the *Reichsarbeitsdienst* hammers symbolised the hammer of Thor ending the dark night of the Weimar soul by building a new dawn for their nation and culture. Their life force energy for the life of the greatest oak forest of them all: the resurrection of the Germanic soul itself.

The Germanic culture which Adolf Hitler grew up in was still very much a repository of stories and legends of witches and monsters haunting the nocturnal landscapes among the forests of trees, and then by osmosis, into the forest of neural pathways which comprised the collective German mind of that era. By the time the embryonic Nazi Party was forming from a turbulent coagulation of Bavarian nationalists, unemployed workers and former military political fringe groups, these aspects of the Germanic personality were still very much held in deeply sequestered partitions within the Teutonic soul. Especially outside the large cities.

Heinrich Himmler, *Reichsführer* of the *Schutzstaffel* or more commonly known as the *SS*, was the most occult-like (on the surface) of Hitler's henchmen, and this came directly from his rural upbringing. Himmler was well aware that beyond the sophisticated suburbs of Munich, Frankfurt and Berlin, and especially within the forests and mountain regions—where millions of Germans lived—was a repository of folklore and superstitions, along with an untapped arsenal of magical and occult archetypes which were as real to the residents of this 'other Germany' as the trees and the rivers around them. However, the 'dark spirits' of the Germanic psychological landscape were often padlocked behind a cage of organised religion, social conformity and educated, civilised modernity. Adolf Hitler, like Himmler, was only too aware of these incarcerated spectres and witches of the archaic pagan forests, and he also had a skeleton key to pick the lock which imprisoned them behind a social veneer of modernity and Christianity. His singular determination was to unleash the demons of the Germanic mind and then distillate them into the material world to bring about the change he desired. In effect, to free Fenrir, son of Loki, from his archetypal and literal captivity and unleash his wrath upon mankind.

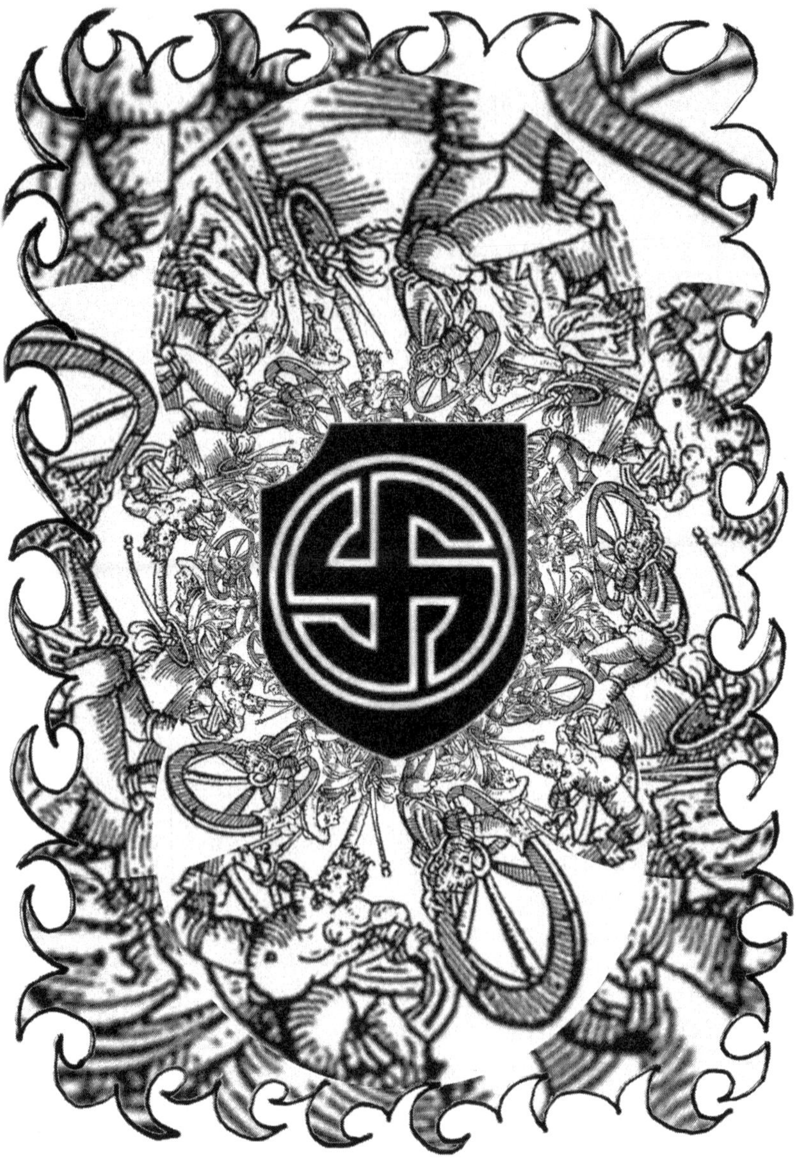

THREE

BURNING TIMES

"Anyone who understands National Socialism only as a political movement knows virtually nothing about it. It is even more than religion, it is the will to a new creation of man."

— Adolf Hitler

To further stress that we are dealing with the rise of an occult order, we must also look to Himmler's desires to rid Germany of the Judeo-Christian spiritual influence, and especially, Catholicism. Of the various branches of Christian faith in Germany, the ordinary Catholics—more than any other congregretion—stood in the way of the Third Reich's Black-Häxan-Paganism revival. German Catholics, unlike the nation's Lutherans (who dispelled the supernatural aspect of their religion after the *Reformation*), were already deeply infused into a rich magical tradition. A supernatural sense of ceremony which had impressed the young Adolf Hitler with its effectiveness to create change in people's consciousness during the *Transubstantiation* of the Catholic mass. He was well aware that it was going to take cunning and craft to deal with the 'Catholic Problem'.

The Holy See had been considered a buffer to German domestic interests long before the arrival of the Nazis. Bismark in the 1870's implemented what was known as *Kulturkampf* ('Cultural Struggle'), a policy directly aimed at Germany's population of practising Roman Catholics. Catholic schooling was banned, the Jesuits expelled, and seminaries and convents constantly subjected to intimidation and harassment. Catholic properties were nationalised, and any member of the Catholic clergy who refused to obey or was outspoken against *Kulturkampf* was hit with massive legal fines, prison terms or deportation. Eventually, the legislation was extended into Switzerland and Austria, having been inspired by intellectuals such as Balzac and Gladstone and their prevailing belief that Catholics had no role to play in modern European life. However, in Germany, this schism went much deeper. The pagan Germanic tribes were still psychologically at war with the Romans in the Black Forest of their subconscious minds, and this vendetta was passed on to ordinary German Catholics; a national trait which the Nazis took full advantage of during their own 'spiritual' crusade.

NEW METHODS OF SORCERY

Hitler was also acutely aware that the archaic folklore and superstitions were rapidly becoming obsolete with the emergence of the 20th century post-Great War society, and in particular, the growth of science and technology. Media, printing technology, the arts and especially the theatre and cinema, all provided a new canon of magic which could be coupled onto the post-agrarian and urban Germanic psyche in order to attain total consciousness domination over both the educated classes, office worker, factory technician and rural farmer alike. Then, as today, the Victorian school of magic which Hitler would have been familiar with (Ariosophy and Theosophy), was becoming obsolete, as the new magi were moving into radio and film production, graphic design and even architecture. Not only in Germany, but everywhere else.

This was the interesting irony surrounding the magical circles and groups flourishing around Europe at that time, such as The Golden Dawn,; in that their systems of magic were becoming rapidly defunct by changes in language brought about by changes in technology and the turbulent cultural shifts of the time. The magic of 1900 was nearly obsolete by 1919, having moved on from the days of The Golden Dawn. The powerful magi were discarding the idea of wearing silly outfits and standing in a circle inside some stately home somewhere. They were becoming scientists and artists as they once were during the heyday of Natural Philosophy.

Adolf Hitler came to the same realisation in the 1920s; that for his 'will' to triumph, his magic would have to be infused with the emerging technology of his age, and especially the rapid advancement in communications technology, rather than carrying along the rituals of the past as they had been performed most probably since the age of antiquity. Everything from electricity to the combustion engine had a part to play in this new school of Nazi sorcery. Even so, the traditional methods of the magical craft were not to be completely discarded as such; rather, they were to be updated. This explains the Third Reich's obsession with astrology, archaic symbolism and runes. Hitler promoted every manner of technological and scientific advancement as complementary aspects of the traditional occult ideas of the time.

As authors such as Dion Fortune and Carl Jung have pointed out in their own psychology and occult work, the use of symbolism affects people at their subconscious level. The reason why people are not conscious of these effects as they happen is due to the subconscious archetypal core of the human mind, being far older than our modern minds, and having evolved before the invention of language and writing. The subconscious mind will understand the symbolism and therefore act upon it. Hence, why the Nazis prominently placed ancient magical insignia and regalia on the latest engineering. Not just confined to military technology and engineering, Hitler also understood the subconscious effects of radio, cinema, music, stagecraft and lighting effects, and even the early forms of television. He then capitalised upon their awesome subconscious potential as contemporary technological conduits into the archaic cores of the target's cognitive functioning. The cathode ray tube as the successor to the alchemical vessel.

Nor was Adolf Hitler alone in doing so at this time in world history. Edward Bernays, the grandson of Sigmund Freud—himself a product of the same decaying and obsolete Austro-Hungarian Empire as Adolf Hitler—took his uncle's understanding of psychoanalysis and subconscious insights into the repressed fears of the human condition to the United States, where he first used it to ironically spellbind the American public into going into the Great War against Germany. Bernays created the image of the German soldier with the Belgian baby on the end of his bayonet, and cast this spell into the consciousness of the decreasingly isolationist American public. After the war, Bernays later created his own empire of public relations, making him one of the most powerful and influential figures in history, succeeding—for the entire course of his life—in his sorcery where Hitler failed. These, and other remarkable synchronicities with uncanny connections to other highly influential figures of the era, followed Hitler all through his life.

WOTAN DESTRUCTION

In much the same manner as Bernays used his own psycho-analytical magic to get Americans to purchase everything from canned fruit to convertibles, Adolf Hitler played on the same fears and inclinations of the German people, unleashing within them powerful, untapped—if not repressed—desires and cultural pathologies. This unshackling of the tamed barbarian just below the civilised exterior is also vitally important in order to perform successful magical rituals on a grand scale. This is the purpose of propaganda and always has been: to reach the primordial, paranoid predator deep inside the human cranium. There are a series of evolutionary 'animals' inside us which are all unfolding outwards from the reptilian complex in our lower brain stems. Hitler became the snake charmer of these future proto-psychopaths who were to slither murderously towards the Slavic world as the viciously efficient and fanatical *SS Einsatzgruppen*; Hitler's most devoted cult followers.

In order to spellbind a target individual or group, the magi must first and foremost create a willing participant. This is why a good stage hypnotist asks for a volunteer from the audience only after scanning/testing the audience for people who can be easily mesmerised. He or she knows well that the more impulsive personality type is the easiest to put into a hypnotic trance, as their subconscious world is closer to the surface than that of the more restrained person. By playing on the superstitions and fears of the Germanic culture—and, in particular, their capacity for envy and arrogance—Adolf Hitler found the perfect volunteers for his craft.

The post-Great War landscape of Germany—a Dante-esque bleakness of broken souls, dreams and hatreds—was the perfect untapped cauldron of neurosis and vindictiveness for an aspiring Black-Häxan-Pagan dictator with unlimited ambition. A fatherless Fatherland simmering with all the fears and all the resentments of a broken people, until the primordial demons of the Germanic soul came out from their hibernation which had previously been sequestered deep within the reptilian complex of the lower brain stem. Like tulpas of tormented souls, they then moved into the upper cerebral partitions with each promise of salvation and restored dignity issued forth, with increasing confidence by the magician Adolf Hitler.

LUTHERANISM AND THE DEVIL

One more factor which plays a major role within the Germanic cultural and social paradox leading up to this part of history—and which needs to be explored in terms of its social impact—is the influence of Martin Luther and the Protestant Reformation upon the collective German psyche. Born in 1483, Luther, the son of a wealthy Catholic family, in time became disillusioned with his faith in much the same way Adolf Hitler himself became disillusioned with Catholicism centuries later.

Not only was Martin Luther the founder of the Protestant faith; he was also a drunken, Jew-hating bigot obsessed with witches and his own personal war with 'devils', whom he claimed was represented on earth by the emissaries of Hell. These devils could destroy crops, cause diseases and create storms. Despising just about anyone who wasn't a German Protestant, Martin Luther viewed Jews especially as nothing other than the *Devil's people*, openly stating this throughout most of his adult life. Luther also believed that there was no such thing as free will, and that all humans were at the mercy of predestination, in that only the will of either God or the Devil determines the life choices and behaviour of all humans. Essentially, Luther was speaking in much the same terms as many geneticists of the present era see humanity: as nothing more than biological robots at the mercy of our DNA, which, ironically, was more or less the same view held by Heinrich Himmler and the *SS*.

Within Lutheranism, God is good, but he allows the Devil to exist within a dualistic framework to weed out the unworthy, or lesser humans. Hence, the Devil is a servant of God, and therefore, necessary. In a cultural sense, this implied that both Catholics, Jews, Gypsies and, centuries later, Marxists, were a necessary evil within Germanic society, as their presence allowed the Nazi administration to weed out the degenerates and the weak who were drawn towards these influences. Luther believed that all his own personal diseases, and his many other ailments—which plagued him during his lifetime—came about as a direct result of Jews and demons attacking him personally. Psychologically, this is fascinating, as it possibly indicates that Luther may have been tormented by the idea that he had a 'Jew inside him'—which needed to be exorcised out—to use a phrase uttered by Himmler. This aspect of National Socialism—removing one's inner Jew—came directly from German Lutheranism.

There are also as many theories surrounding Martin Luther's mother potentially having a sexual relationship with a Jewish merchant as there are that Adolf Hitler himself having a Jewish grandfather. In the case of Hitler, it is now considered highly unlikely that Hitler had a Jewish grandfather. However—and this is highly important to understanding the psychology of both Martin Luther and Adolf Hitler—according to Robert G. L. Waite in his book, *The Psychopathic*

God Adolf Hitler, the fear of the possibility of having Jewish blood flowing through his veins created a psychopathic neurosis within Hitler which manifested outwardly into irrational hatreds. This same self-loathing brought about by cryptic or paranoid genealogy was almost certainly a factor in Martin Luther's own theological world view.

Where this all gets really interesting is when we couple this with Martin Luther's pathological obsession with witchcraft and his own personal battles with the Lord of Darkness. He blamed his wild mood swings and depression—while he translated the Bible into German—on demons and witches with an almost equal revulsion to that of his hatred for Jews.

He once stated, "I should have no compassion on these witches. I would burn all of them. We read in the old law that the priests threw the first stones at these malefactors...Does not witchcraft, then, merit death, which is a revolt of the creature against the Creator, a denial to God of the authority which it accords to the demon?" Notice that Luther's main neurosis concerning witchcraft is based around submission to authority, the rule or law and the will of something he called 'the Creator'. The 'Creator', in esoteric terms, is not necessarily the God of the Old Testament—the psychopathic, blood-thirsty, lion-faced, demiurge named Jehovah—and is also a term used by

Freemasons to denote another deity, which in Masonry is Lucifer, *the Light Bringer*. Martin Luther was a deeply paradoxical individual in terms of his theology, and may even have been a secret Satanist himself, more at war with the Holy See than reforming Christianity back to a more Gnostic idea. Hitler and the Nazis, on the other hand, threw out all Christianity and placed their weaponised version of Black-Häxan-Paganism at the central core of their ideology. This would have been a very appealing offering to a Germany still divided by the after-effects of the *Protestant Reformation* and uninspired by the spiritually facile cul-de-sac of the *Enlightenment*.

Although Martin Luther wrote extensive polemics on the nature of witchcraft, there is, however, an important distinction pertaining to the actual school of magic he was in conflict with at the time, in that he may not have been referring directly to Teutonic Magic or Häxan-Pagan rituals. These older Nordic systems of folk magic had been mostly eliminated during the late Middle Ages within much of Germany, and was by the time of the *Reformation* consigned mainly to fairy tales and folklore until the revival of the Teutonic Magic or Häxan-Pagan tradition in the mid- to late-Victorian era. At the time of Luther's crusade against witches and devils, another system of magic from the Slavic world was moving into Bavaria and Saxony from the East.

The cult of Veles (or Volos) had merged into the Teutonic supernatural framework via the ethnic Germanic populations in Bohemia, Poland, the Balkans and Romania. Veles is the Slavic magical force of nature, and is found present in the landscape, waterways and in the Slavic version of Hell. Veles is the deity of dragons, livestock, bears, sorcery, artists, and commerce. Veles is the opponent of the Supreme thunder-god Perun (among Germans, this would have been Donar or Thor, who, interestingly, is almost identical to the Vedic thunder god Indra from the ancestral land of the swastika, India), and the war between Veles and Perun (Thor) represents the central focus of Slavic folk magic.

Starting with the *Battle of Munich* in April/May 1919 and continuing with *Operation Barbarossa* during the Second World War, the struggle between National Socialism and Marxism can be reduced down to the archetypal level to the earthly manifestation of a mythology conflict between Wotan and Veles via the 19th century distillation created by the rise of Theosophy and Ariosophy, which themselves were previously expressed by the rise of Lutheranism and its phobia of other religious and occult forces.

Clearly, we can see from this that the agitation between the Teutons and the Slavs took place in the 'heavens' and the 'underworld' (in terms of manifestations of the psyche) long before Hitler conjured up his *Lebensraum* principle to rid the East of Slavs (along with Veles). At the time of Martin Luther, and in the years following his *Protestant Reformation*, this Slavic system of magic would have been his main concern in terms of witchery, as it would have arrived with the 'devils' in tandem with the migration of Jews who were also moving into Germany from the East at that point in history.

Traditionally, Jews and 'witches' were persecuted and murdered in Germany during the same round-ups, and regular scapegoating of both groups by the authorities. Burning Jews was considered an opportunity to also burn 'witches' at the same time, and vice versa. The ensuing mayhem was often used to seize properties and holdings belonging to the victims, a tactic later implemented by the Nazis during the invasion of Poland in 1939, as the *SS-Polizei-Bataillone* committed atrocities against both the Catholic and the Jewish populations with the vacated properties given to ethnic Germans living on Polish territories. There was nothing new in what Hitler and Third Reich implemented; the only difference being the colossal industrial scale of the manifested hatred. The same basic template remained.

Luther issued other polemics which were to hugely saturate the Germanic consciousness in the centuries to come, and which were also to make the national revival of the Black-Häxan-Paganism of the Nazis even more seamless. This was Luther's obsession with German women and purity of German blood. He believed that maidens were seduced by *devils* (Jews, Catholics and Slavs) by giving them warm baths, and then, the seductive, demonic males would impregnate them, and the children born to these women would be of a similar status as the 'changelings' of European folk traditions. In this context, these children would not be fully German.

Later, this fear of 'devils' blood corrupting the women of Germany would be rebranded by the *SS* as the *Lebensborn* (Fount of Life) Aryan breeding programme. More disturbingly, one has to speculate if the *SS Einsatzgruppen*, as they slaughtered their way from the Polish border to Stalingrad, were (psycho-culturally) murdering witches and 'devils' and burning them—without Lutheran 'compassion'—having been culturally pre-programmed to do so from their social and even genetic memory of their ancestors?

The last sermon given by Martin Luther on February 15, 1564 was against the Jews and devils. He died three days later, believing that these forces of darkness had struck him down. Four hundred years later, the Wannsee Conference, which was chaired by *SS-Obergruppenführer* Reinhard Heydrich, so as to implement the Final Solution, whereby most of the remaining Jews of Nazi-occupied Europe would be deported to Poland for extermination, took place under a Nazi regime which had most of Europe under its boot. Ultimately, it was a culmination of Martin Luther's belief in a necessary Devil, manifesting, ironically, as a Black-Häxan-Paganism continuum. The flywheel of history does not cease when the engine that first set it into motion has been switched off. The energy contained within its mass carries on through the ages.

München
1919

FOUR

IMMORTAL COMBAT

"The blood-dimmed tide is loosed, and everywhere

The ceremony of innocence is drowned"

— William Butler Yeats (1919)

When you ask people what the most significant date during the 20th century was, very few of them would reply that it was April 30, 1919. On the morning of *Walpurgis Night*, when an incredibly stupid and callous act was carried out by the predominantly Jewish-Bolshevik 'Spartacist' leadership of the Bavarian Soviet Republic in Munich, ordering members of the Red Guards to execute eleven people, some of whom were well-connected members of the Thule Society by firing squad on false and wildly trumped-up charges. The Red Guards fired dum-dum rounds into the innocent victims lined up against a wall in a schoolyard, which literally caused the targets' bodies to explode, including that of a well-liked Jewish college professor, whose crime was tearing down a Bolshevik propaganda poster, and, most significantly of all, two high-ranking members of the Thule Society named Prince von Thurn und Taxis and Countess von Westarp.

The Thule Society was an occult organisation based on a legend of an ancient Nordic civilisation which once lived inside the earth, and by 1919, the Thulists had managed to develop an organisation of surprisingly impressive resources and influence. Apart from conducting seances, magical rituals and other rites one would expect of such an organisation, the Thule Society was also very politically active, with their main focus being on organising militia groups and propaganda against the Spartacist movement, which took root in Germany at the end of the Great War. No sooner than the bodies of the executed been taken from the school gymnasium, that highly organised and well-trained Prussian *Freikorps,* in tandem with an occult paramilitary force named the Thule Combat League, were descending upon the Bavarian city to crush the local Soviet revolution.

Immediately upon hearing of the executions, the Thule Combat League drove into the suburbs of Munich on trucks, armoured cars and captured British tanks from the Somme, emblazoned with the Skull and Crossbones and other occult symbols painted on their radiator grills and, most significantly of all, members of the *Freikorps* and Thule Combat League had hastily painted swastikas and runic symbols on their helmets. The world would never be the same again, as the events of *Walpurgis Night/May Day* 1919 were to change the course of human history forever. Among the Thule Combat League fighters arriving in Munich that morning was a semi-aristocratic occultist named Rudolf Hess.

By all accounts, 1919 was a year when pathological and sometimes well-intentioned political forces made their opportunistic grab for power in the wake of the calamity that was the Great War. What was proclaimed to be the first year of stability and peace following the 'War to End All Wars'—which ritualistically ended on the eleventh hour, of the eleventh day, of the eleventh month—became anything but that. The turbulence following the Great War and all during the so-called 'Paris Peace Conference' at the Palace of Versailles, became little more than combustive forces of vindictiveness and old score settling, which were placed next to a burning candle of resentment and inter-ethnic tensions. All it was going to take was a strong wind of change to detonate the terrifying power waiting to be unleashed.

That year, the roll call of revolutions and uprisings seemed neverending. The first Irish Parliament had assembled in Dublin, brazenly declaring an Irish Republic which resulted in a war between Ireland and Great Britain. Wars also broke out between Poland and the Soviet Union, as well as Estonia and the Soviet Union, while

Czechoslovakia and Romania made territorial land grabs to expand their national borders. There were major uprisings in Mexico, Argentina, Egypt, Hungary, the Ukraine, Moldova and India. 1919 was also the year that Benito Mussolini founded the Italian Fascist Party in Milan, and there were major political disturbances from the steel mills and shipyards of the United States to the coal mines and linen factories of Scotland.

In that same year, the League of Nations was founded; an ill-designed, doomed bureaucratic blueprint for the perpetuation of never-ending conflict that was set in motion as basically a survival plan for imperialist structures posing as a global peace and cooperation body. 1919 and the calamities that saturated each month of that calendar year were a culmination of what today we would call 'think-tanks' and 'policy steering groups', made up of mainly British, French and American aristocrats who had set up their grand chess pieces in the decades leading up to *Walpurgis Night*, 1919.

THE FABIAN CHESSBOARD

One organisation that was very influential on the global stage and whose actions and implementations directly led to the rise of the totalitarianism of both Fascism and the Bolsheviks was the Fabian Society. Based in London and formed in 1884, and which still exists and remains influential in global politics to the present day, this think-tank was and still is essentially an aristocratic cult out, of which which formed the British Labour Party, the London School of Economics and the influential *New Statesman* journal, as well as having a huge influence on the creation of the League of Nations in 1919.

The Fabian ideology is driven by incremental social Darwinism and scientific socialism, and until the 1940's did nothing to hide their totalitarian psychopathic agenda. In fact, they openly boasted about their horrific agenda which, today, is now hidden behind a façade of celebrities and climate change fronts. The same aristocratic families which championed the ethos and rise of both National Socialism and the Bolsheviks are very much still moving the Fabian rudder and maintaining their utopian course behind the scenes just as much as they ever have as you read these very words.

The Irish playwright George Bernard Shaw was a Fabian who openly called for scientists to develop gasses to murder races and groups who did not want to be controlled within the Fabian utopia. Later, IG Faben would cater to his wishes with their 'pesticide' Zyklon B; poured upon European Gypsies, in an attempt to eliminate the last non-controlled indigenous people in Europe. Shaw also demanded a system whereby humans were to sit in front of a committee and justify their existence to a panel of civil servants who had the right to decide a person's fate. If people could no longer demonstrate that they were productive before this panel of bureaucrats, they would be 'humanely murdered' according to George Bernard Shaw.

The influence that the Fabians had on the creation of National Socialism and the Bolsheviks cannot be downplayed, as they were significant in generating a degree of acceptance of totalitarian regimes among intellectuals and academics in the years leading up to 1919. Hitler and Stalin could not have risen to power without the social conditioning of the Fabians; that a cold, scientific control of humanity was the only method of government for the 20th century. The Fabian Society was ruthlessly atheistic and scientific, and this was perhaps what made them so very dangerous, in that they assumed that human existence is nothing more than chemical and electrical bodily functions, and that humanity has no soul or spirit.

Later, Adolf Hitler, during his rise to power, was aware that just because a scientist says that the supernatural does not exist, does not mean that the supernatural is still not a powerful force of the human experience. Hitler knew magic was real, because unlike the Fabians and their materialist fellow travellers, Hitler fully understood how powerful a tool magic is, and he used it to attain access to the core of human cognition that the scientist had no idea even existed. The

Fabians gave the Third Reich their social policy licence from which to hide their Black-Häxan-Pagan revival behind.

DARK THINGS TO COME

Among the more psychopathic—if not psychotic—members of the Fabian Society who used his popular influence to sow the seeds of the totalitarian scientific oppression in the name of reason, was the British author H.G. Wells. Known mainly for using his science-fiction novels such as *The Time Machine* and *Things to Come* in order to future-proof the expectations of present generations towards political objectives (which is why sci-fi remains a core aspect of the Psychopathic Control Grid to this day), Wells and his warped philosophy played a huge part in the creation of both Hitler and Stalin in terms of their acceptability among more scientifically inclined thinkers in the decades leading up to 1919.

H.G. Wells was not only a vicious anti-Semite; he also despised Catholics, and hated those humans who were not completely controlled and organised according to the Ulster Loyalist Presbyterian world view he had been raised in. Wells was perhaps the most perfectly pre-formed National Socialist who wasn't a German. Like so many of the intelligentsia of his day, he took Charles Darwin's *survival of the fittest* concept to a completely literal level, in that some humans were just not fit to live in the scientific and reasoned *New Order* of the 20th century that he and the other Fabians had envisioned.

Wells, carrying the ethos of the Fabians into a literary narrative, declared that 'The Base' of humanity was unfit to live because, culturally and intellectually, their need to be free and have free will had to be removed from society as 'congenital invalids', as they only represented 'an antagonism to the State organisations.' His solution, as was also that of the Fabians, was for the Utopians to eliminate 'The Base'.

This was to be achieved by means of mass starvation and robbing these people of both their ability to survive and their will to live. Precisely the same methods used by the Nazis with the Nuremberg Racial Laws and which led to the 'silent holocaust', whereby Jews and others declared unfit to live in the Reich chose suicide in their countless thousands as they were shunned, made unemployed or mocked and chased out of schools and universities. The Nazis adopted these methods directly from H.G. Wells and the other British intellectuals of the Fabian Society. There is no difference at all between H.G. Wells' 'congenital invalids' and Adolf Hitler's 'racial tuberculosis'. The same use of weaponised black magic language was being unleashed to create pre-formed opinions in the minds of their audience, while at the same time serving notice to the victims that 'the hunt is on'.

H.G. Wells' elimination of 'The Base' classes included forbidding the undesirables from building boats, as islands off the coast were to be used as concentration camps while the Utopians arranged their extermination. Just like the Nazis, Wells and the Fabians demanded that malformed children and disabled adults should be murdered, as they would affect the finances of the state and may contaminate the bloodlines of the Utopians with malformed strains. Wells (on behalf of the Fabian Society) demanded uniformity of attire and uniformed clothing, that all marriages be arranged and decreed by the state with total bureaucratic control of family diets and recreational facilities.

As incredible as it seems, this was the prevailing mindset of the British and Anglo-American establishment in the first half of the 20th century, and without fully understanding this period of history, whereby the Scientific Materialists proposed their own form of National Socialism for the world and then unleashed everything from Eugenics to Gerrymandering, we cannot begin to grasp why the Anglo-American establishment became so enamoured with Adolf Hitler and the Nazis during their rise to power. In many ways, Hitler was the Fabians' ideal leader in Berlin, just as much as Lenin and later Stalin were their ideal leadership culture in Moscow. This happened because the imperial powers following the Great War—even if only by fostering a culture of acceptability—created the means for it to have happened.

THE DEMON-MENTORED EMIGRE

Another hero of late Victorian/Edwardian intellectuals and who, much like George Bernard Shaw and H.G. Wells were considered paragons of reason and common sense at the time, was the British author Houston Stewart Chamberlain. A Darwinian social climber, he was an English author of books on philosophy and natural sciences. Chamberlain married the composer Richard Wagner's daughter, Eva von Bülow and became a German citizen. In 1899, Chamberlain authored the highly influential book, *The Foundations of the Nineteenth Century* (*Die Grundlagen des neunzehnten Jahrhunderts*), which became the guidebook for the emerging *völkisch* racial-blood group movements. In effect, the British elite were instructing the Germans on how to be consumed and obsessed with their own blood and racial superiority in order to radicalise them into anti-Semitism with the aim of cultivating large scale emigration of European Jewry to Palestine. Chamberlain's agenda went hand in hand with the British Israelite movement—comprised mainly of British and Irish hardcore Protestants—of the same era which created Zionism, in order to manufacture an Ulster-style political situation in the Middle East, serving British imperialist objectives. What makes Houston Stewart Chamberlain so interesting is that he seems to have become possessed by his own statesmanship, in that what started as British imperialist objectives he came to believe and become obsessed by. His constant proximity to Richard Wagner—an instinctual magician of awesome power, it has to be said—captivated Chamberlain to the point where he became a sort of British pre-Hitler. Eventually, Chamberlain stated that only the Teutonic races were worthy of being called either civilised and cultured.

In tandem with the British Israelite movement, Chamberlain was one of the first 'serious' authors to give credence to the idea that Jesus Christ was a blond, blue-eyed Nordic aristocrat. If that wasn't enough, Chamberlain also claimed that his writings and insights were channelled from demons who instructed him in how to develop his ideas and theories. Chamberlain became the German Kaiser's mystical advisor, and eagerly pushed the German government into the Great War. His bitter disappointment at Germany's failure to control Europe at the end of the Great War was finally resolved when he encountered Adolf Hitler in 1923 and declared him the Aryan god who would deliver the blood of the Nordic races back to its rightful place as the rulers of the earth. The demons inside Chamberlain never stopped whispering into his ear.

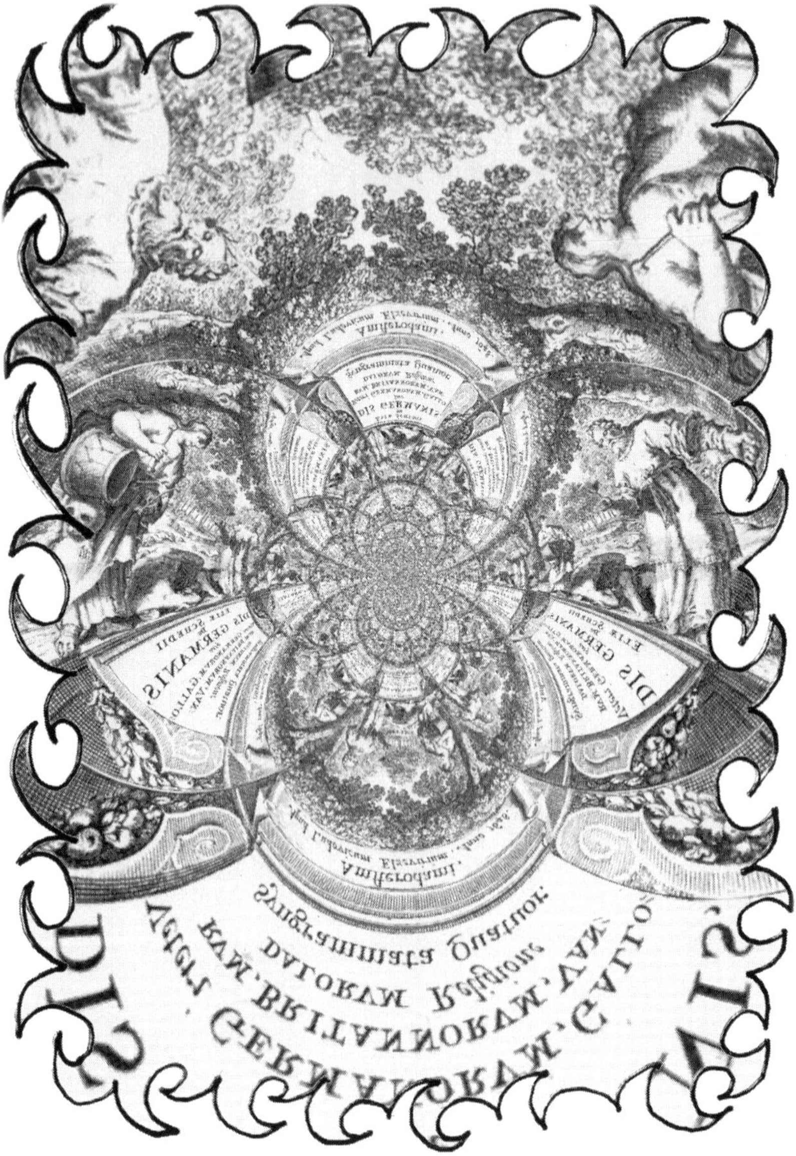

FIVE

BROKEN WALLS

"It is forbidden to kill; therefore all murderers are punished unless they kill in large numbers and to the sound of trumpets."

— Voltaire

As the pieces on the grand imperial chess board of the global powers moved into their final position during the closing months of the post-Great War power play, it was becoming more apparent that 1919 was turning out to be the year that changed the world forever. It was also the year that the German psyche was to unleash the demons of the Teutonic mind, and the world would never be the same again. Germany, more than anywhere else, was to experience the full convulsive aftermath of the *'War to End All Wars'*: politically, socially, psychologically and culturally. Germany was left a damaged nation and, like any dying creature, the infections began to multiply and spread as the emotional and economic immune system of the nation began to deteriorate with terrifying speed. Try to imagine yourself in the Germany of that time, or the Weimar Republic as it had been renamed. A once proud and powerful people—who were always more of a racial and linguistic tribe than a unified national force—reduced to the status of a slave state in the aftermath of a war they didn't actually lose. German cities and towns still would have looked architecturally similar to how they did in the Middle Ages, now with a new era of modern poverty and hopelessness everywhere. While the rest of the world spoke of new beginnings and bright futures, the German people were essentially transported back to the time of great plagues, wicked rulers, fairytale monsters and the black arts.

The façade of modernity and civilisation was no longer present, as a constricting shadow moved across the land from the Baltic to the Alps. Such landscapes are fertile grounds for the gestation of monsters and ritual magic. Not just in Germany itself, but also within the Germanic hinterland of Austria, as the last vestige of a once mighty empire was being strangled into neurosis and stagnation by the purposeful madness implanted by the Treaty of Versailles.

MAYHEM, MURDER AND MAGIC IN MUNICH

In January 1919, the Spartacist uprising led by Communists suddenly ignited within Berlin and other German cities. A Marxist Jewess from Poland named Rosa Luxembourg—who was instrumental in the political formation of the Weimar Republic—initially discouraged her followers from taking part in this violent attempt to create a German Soviet. Nevertheless, she appears to have encouraged Spartacist radicals to seize newspaper and other media offices. This led to outrage among many Germans who felt it was a betrayal of those who died fighting the now Soviet Russians on the Eastern Front.

In reprisal, the Social Democratic leader Friedrich Ebert ordered the *Freikorps*—well organised and violent groups of mostly former soldiers who were to later become the early core of Hitler's *SA* Brownshirts—to take down the Marxist uprising which they did with ruthless brutality.

Rosa Luxembourg, along with her lover Karl Liebknecht—who was one of the founders of the Communist Party of Germany (KDP)—were arrested in Berlin on 15 January 1919 by the *Freikorps' Garde-Kavallerie-Schützendivision*. Luxembourg was then interrogated, beaten, shot and her body thrown into Landwehr Canal. In the Tiergarten, Karl Liebknecht was shot and his body was dumped in the local morgue and left unidentified. The instant brutality of the killings shocked the German nation, and this then incensed the more extreme left-wing elements into further revolt and conflict. Germany was on the brink of all-out civil strife to compound the everyday hopelessness of the post-Great War misery.

Following the murders of Luxembourg and Liebknecht, major violence flared up all over the country, as heavily armed and well-trained *Freikorps* easily overcame the KPD in several major street battles. Thousands of communists and other revolutionaries were subjected to mass summary executions. Disturbances took place all over Germany until early summer, with heavy fighting taking place in Berlin, Hamburg, and finally, leading to the defeat of the Bavarian Soviet Republic, which was annihilated by the *Freikorps* on May 2, 1919. Again, the *Freikorps* were in no mood to take prisoners and the streets of Munich ran red with blood.

Germany in 1919 was still being torn asunder by the psychic shell-shock of the Great War, as millions of Germans went deeper into their primoridal minds looking for answers, escape and refuge among their subconscious archetypal allies, which could not only help these traumatised Germans to express their national sense of torment and hopelessness, but also to provide the means from which to escape it. Little did they or the world know that the demons and ghosts of the primordial Teutonic underworld were already moving out from the darkest woodlands and coming down from their caves in the remote mountain passes looking for their agents and the soon-to-be-possessed. While the Bavarian Soviet Republic was being created in a maelstrom of blood and repression, a group of occultists and arms runners were directing the counter-insurgency operation from a nearby hotel, and this cabal of violent magicians and how they functioned were to become the curtain raiser for what was to follow in the years ahead, when Adolf Hitler was to be invited in as their 'guest'.

EVERY SUPERIOR MAN AND WOMAN IS A STAR

H.G. Wells and his use of science fiction to provisionally create a future according to the needs of a control structure was the default means of future-proofing global social and technological changes by the end of the Great War. The Fabians used science fiction to ready the population to accept the 'inevitable' as the agenda was unfolding. This form of predictive magic was spawned from and within similar social circles that also created the 19th century occult revival. In 1871, a novel by a Rosicrucian named Edward Bulwer-Lytton entitled, *Vril, the Power of the Coming Race,* is perhaps the first work of science fiction designed to generate a sense of expectation within readers, in that the storyline itself would eventually come to pass. The narrative being presented is not a fantasy, but rather a blueprint of what is, and what is to come. Influential occult figures such as Helena Blavatsky and Rudolf Steiner, along with other Theosophists, claimed that the book's narrative of a master race living inside a hollow earth who possess the power of an energy form which they called Vril was rooted in fact.

In the story, a young adventurer discovers a subterranean civilisation of angelic Aryan-looking beings called the Vril-ya. The Vril-ya, who were once human, went to live inside the earth before the Great Flood as described in the *Bible*. Their cities are linked by networks of tunnels in which they create technological 'wonders'. This narrative of *Vril, the Power of the Coming Race*, eventually became culturally, if not esoterically infused within Nazi ideology, as later, the Third Reich—along with their secret weapons development programmes—basically went underground into bunkers and tunnels inside mountains after 1942 in order to design and build their 'V' weapons.

However, the one aspect of Edward Bulwer-Lytton's novel which really captured the imagination of occultists of the time such as the Order of the Templars and Thule Society in Germany, was the energy force of the Vril-ya; the "all-permeating fluid" of Vril, which the Ariosophists took to mean Aryan blood. A force, if kept pure and free from being contaminated by other inferior blood races, could unleash incredible psychic and energetic forces according to the training of one's will. This included telepathy and wonder weapons which could wipe out entire cities. The suggestion is made in the novel that the

Vril-ya will eventually return to the surface of the earth if a pure racial Aryan blood group evolves on the surface of the planet, taking with them their awesome magical powers and sharing these powers with the surface Aryan master race. The idea so excited members of the Thule Society that they formed a group in Berlin called *Wahrheitsgesellschaft*, or The Society for Truth, which was charged with discovering the power of Vril and using it to create wonder weapons.

Although this was a fictional novel, it was taken very literally as fact by many intellectuals of the time; not just in Germany, but also in the United States and significantly, in the UK, where similar ideas of racial magic were being developed—fusing science fiction and Eugenics as a necessary destiny for mankind to aspire towards, or perish. The underlying theme was always the same: that the tall, blond, blue-eyed and fair-skinned races were the inheritors of the earth, and they will be forever in danger as long as dark and ape-like humans continue to multiply. This created a phobia among the upper echelons of society of impending extinction 'of their superior kind' before the Vril-ya, or a similar magical race arrives to evolve the earthly master races into the next stage of evolution.

THE COMING OF THE NEW ORDER

The Thule Combat League, which was entering Munich during the *Witches Sabbath* in April 1919, was the culmination of several decades of gradual magical and occult revivals that had taken root not just in Germany but also in Europe and North America. Irish occultists of the Golden Dawn, which included W.B. Yeats, Lady Gregory and A.E. Russell, had successfully fused the *Gaelic Revival* in Ireland to inspire the Irish independence movement via Republican occultists such as Maud Gonne, while Aleister Crowley, fresh from working as a double agent among German sympathisers in New York, had a mystical vision of developing his Abbey of Thelema in Mussolini's Fascist Italy and starting his new religion. *The Spiritualist Movement* in the United States—which had even penetrated into the inner core of the White House—was as popular as ever, inspiring American radio and telegraph engineers to develop machines to communicate with the spirits of the dead.

All of these movements were a reaction to the loss of traditional folk cultures, along with the diminishing spiritual influence of the Protestant religions among the middle and upper classes, who still retained a powerful conviction for the supernatural in the face of the industrial and scientific revolutions. Germany was the one place where the veneer of the repressed Dark Druids below the surface had the thinnest layer of modernity holding it back.

ORDER OF THE HOLY SWASTIKA

In 1909, Dr. Jorg Lanz von Leibenfels—a former member of the Order of the Holy Cross—hoisted a flag above the ruined castle at Wefenstein in Austria where his new esoteric order was operating from at the time. The image on the flag was the swastika. Lanz von Leibenfels then led his cult members in a series of chants in honour of Teutonic racial purity towards the constellations of the night skies as the flag, which would cast such a deep shadow over the human experience, was flown for the first time. Having spent some time developing the swastika as a sigil of racial magic until the design invoked the specific imagery he felt comfortable with, Dr. Lanz von Leibenfels created a combination of the hammer of Thor in perpetual motion, coupled with previous versions of the swastika graphic which had already been around for hundreds of years in numerous spiritual traditions, including stone-carved swastikas adorning ancient Jewish synagogues in Palestine.

It was a typical cult compound situation for the Order of the Templars at Wefenstein, as the members read the manifestos of their leader with titles such as *Theo-zoology* and *Electronic God*. In the modern age, cults generally publish articles or run alternative 'news' websites which are clandestine fronts for attracting new recruits. The idea is to provide just enough common sense to get everyone looking at the content, but then add a specific amount of 'esoteric flavouring' in order to target the specific type of individual the cult needs to recruit into their ranks. Back in 1909 it was no different than it is today, with the proliferation of alien contactee and comet death cults fishing for potential members on the Internet, except back then it was via newsletters and pamphlets published by the cults and which were then distributed among the general public. Sold for a modest price at tobacconist shops, these pamphlets also provided the cults with a steady income and diverse readership.

Lanz von Leibenfels' main publication was a journal under the name of *Ostara,* named after the German *Goddess of Spring* (based initially on Isis). The same 'Goddess' that Hitler would invoke over and over again and all through his life, and which he claimed ruled over his fate. In 1951, Lanz von Leibenfels was interviewed by a German journalist, and he admitted that one afternoon a young Adolf Hitler came to the Wefenstein cult compound looking for back issues of *Ostara*, which were missing from his personal collection. Lanz von Leibenfels claims he gave Hitler the missing issues for free, as he felt sorry for him and that he seemed so taken with the publication and its content. Within the pages of *Ostara*, there were articles that contained what Lanz von Leibenfels termed '*Fraja-Christus*' or the new Aryan Jesus of the coming order. This obviously influenced the young Hitler enormously, especially the articles entitled *Sexual-Physics as Odylic Energy*. This directable magical force had been identified by Baron Carl von Reichenbach half a century before, who named the force as a tribute to the Norse god Odin. Hitler was later to demonstrate a knowledge of what is commonly known today as *Sex Magic* when his star began to rise, and women lined up to offer themselves sexually to him. These women would be emotionally and sexually damaged by their *Sex Magic* encounters with Hitler, and suicide was not uncommon among them. As cults generally target young, damaged and misguided idealistic people—'idealism' being just another term for 'fascism' when you think about it—it is perhaps not surprising that they would discover the young Adolf Hitler arriving at their doorstep. For the former monk who had walked away from the Christian church and created his own sect in a run-down castle on the banks of the Danube, Lanz von Leibenfels inside his demonic citadel would have been a natural magnet for any aspiring '*Fraja-Christus*'.

The attraction of the castle is another interesting factor, as cults—according to a Muslim friend of mine—need large houses, castles and chateaus in order to house the large number of 'Djinn' (demons) who tend to nest among these cults. These demonic entities are said to be drawn to such environments—filled with amateur magicians, damaged and vulnerable persons at the mercy of a central psychopathic leadership 'family' structure—in order for the Djinn to develop a nest of mind parasites within the consciousness of certain broken people: naive and lost souls who are getting involved in rituals unaware of the potential psychic dangers which can be unleashed, as the cult members are just looking for answers to their own personal problems, rather than these lost souls embarking on a sincere magical quest for enlightenment.

If, as some people have suggested that Hitler may well have been possessed by a demonic entity, then the cult compound at Wefenstein would have been the most likely location for this to have taken place, as Hitler was at his most psychically and emotionally vulnerable during this time. Assuming that such an entity did exist and took control of Adolf Hitler, then perhaps this was the voice which seemed to communicate with Hitler for the rest of his life while he reportedly muttered and screamed in terror during his legendary long periods of sleep alone in his locked room? Often emerging from these sessions with ambitious new plans, solutions to seemingly insurmountable problems and fresh orders were given to his staff and military. This also serves to demonstrate the personality distinctions between Adolf Hitler and the person who would later become his closest friend and future *Deputy Führer,* Rudolf Hess.

Socially, they were both very different. More importantly, Hess had a serious occult background and history which is open and well known. It is not unfeasable that Hess may well have been charged with being the Aryan John the Baptist to Adolf Hitler's *'Fraja-Christus'*. Incredibly, Rudolf Hess, who was born and raised in Egypt, developed his interest in the occult at the same time as Aleister Crowley—who was also in Egypt—when the *Great Beast 666* heard the voice of Aiwass, the messenger telling Crowley that humanity was entering a new Aeon, and that Crowley would serve as the prophet of the *Age of Horus*. Eventually, Crowley and Hitler's paths would cross with the arrival of the Second World War.

Years later, as he sat in a military convoy adorned with occult symbols, little did Rudolf Hess know that while on his way to Munich on the *Witches Sabbath* of *Walpurgis Night* 1919—as a front line soldier in the Thule Combat League—that his own destiny was about to begin and amazingly, the one high-ranking Nazi we can clearly point to regarding his occult history who would outlive them all before being murdered by the Anglo-American occultists who were still terrified of his legendary status and longevity. Even when he was an old man of 93, crippled with arthritis, interned as the only inmate inside Spandau prison carrying some of the most powerful secrets of the 20th century to his grave.

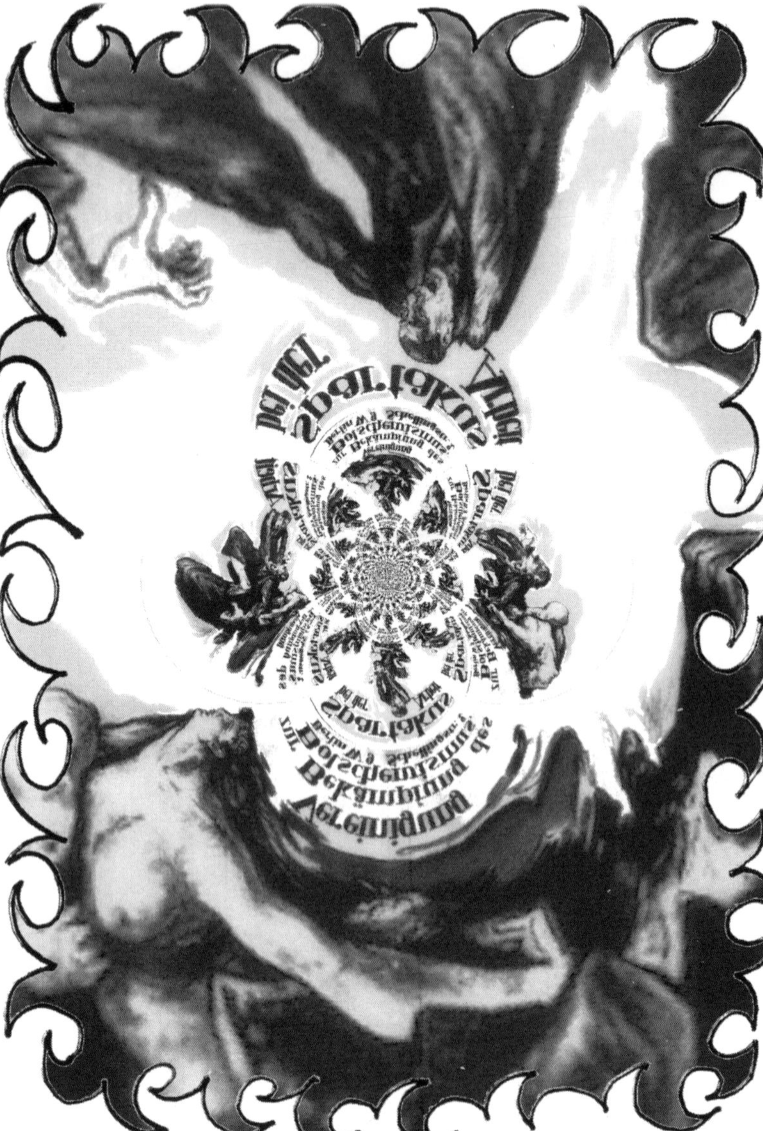

SIX

BLOOD BROTHERS AND SISTERS

"If the doors of perception were cleansed, every thing would appear to man as it is—infinite. For man has closed himself up, till he sees all things through narrow chinks of his cavern."

— William Blake

Following the chaos of the *Palm Sunday Putsch,* when the Thule Society provided the *Freikorps* with free train tickets and weapons in order to get them into Munich to fight with Red Guard factions who were attempting to set up a Bavarian Soviet Republic, gangs of young Russians of mainly Jewish background living in Munich at the time, saw the chaos as a chance to set up a Second Bolshevik dictatorship in the city. The leader of these revolutionaries was the Bavarian Communist Party chairman Eugen Leviné, and no sooner had this faction taken control of the city than they implemented a ruthless Marxist regime of murder and oppression.

Confiscation of businesses and bank accounts and collectivisation of local industries were first on the agenda as armed Marxist thugs ran riot throughout the city, implementing the traditional Communist revolutionary doctrines of brutal ideological oppression and murdering anyone they felt like killing according to Lenin-Trotsky 'scientific' terror tactics. The agenda was to be always unleashed in the wake of a Soviet revolution, so as to terrorise the rest of the population into compliance. Curfews, summary executions and interrogations to announce the usual 'workers revolution' by the typical middle- and upper-class Marxists, most of whom had never been inside a factory or coal mine in their lives. Among these was close ally of Lenin and a Bolshevik fanatic named Max Levien, who arrived in Bavaria to order the proletariat to die for the revolution, and who was also constantly issuing death sentences on members of the Munich bourgeoisie.

Something of a bourgeoisie himself, Max Levien—like all fanatical socialists, and Marxists—had less in common with the working classes he purported to be liberating than the aristocrats he claimed to hate. The demons of the *Old Testament* polluted his Demiurge-infected consciousness, demanding sacrifice and blood. George Bernard Shaw and the other Fabian aristocrats back in London were looking at the 'Red Terror' unleashed in Munich approvingly, as Max Levien and the other intellectuals of the Bavarian Soviet Republic boasted about starving bourgeoisie babies in Munich to death by denying them milk. As mandates were arrogantly issued via their Russian accents and mannerisms, Munich became something akin to *The Book of Leviticus*, and in many ways this is precisely what it was.

However, the one notorious act that the fanatical and tyrannical Max Levien—who still remains a hero figure among leftist college professors within *OxBridge* circles, and who enjoys hero status among contemporary political cults such as the Socialist Workers' Party to this day—was his order to have seven members of the Thule Society put up against a wall and shot on April 30, 1919. From this act of cold-blooded murder, Levien (indirectly) gave the Nazis the 'justification' they needed—when they rose to power—in order to blame and punish all Jews, Marxists and Russians as a collective adversarial entity, for the crimes of Levien and the Red Guards in Munich on that day.

THE AEON BEGINS IN MUNICH

The Thule Society was not so different in some ways from the many esoteric covens and sects found all over Europe at that time. Its membership was drawn mostly from local pseudo-intellectuals, artists and occultists, while the group was publicly declaring itself as nothing more than a literary and philosophical club. Meeting at the luxurious Four Seasons Hotel in central Munich, the Thule Society was anything but a harmless discussion group. It was a subversive, politically powerful and culturally-influencing force to be reckoned with. The Society even had its own paramilitary wing, which played a major part in the public executions of the members of the failed Soviet coup in the city when scores of Marxists were placed into pits and machine-gunned as they pointed to their wedding rings sobbing, and begging for their lives. The realisation that they had been duped by the Bolshevik emissaries of the demiurgic 'creator' arriving from the east, came too late to save them. These very public executions—which were more akin to death rituals—were witnessed by many future Nazis enjoying the spectacles of slaughter as they harvested the dark energy unleashed.

Along with supplying weapons and organising safe houses for 'knights', the Thule Society also flooded Bavaria with anti-Semitic literature. On the morning of the Teutonic *Witches Sabbath*, almost certainly the date selected by Levien in order to infuriate the Thule Society as well as the traditional conservatives of Germany, two prominent members of the German establishment, along with nine other randomly taken prisoners were put up against a wall and shot by the gunmen of the Red Guards. Most were picked up by Red Guards after raiding the Thule Society's operations headquarters at the Four Seasons Hotel after they had been tipped off by a waiter working there. The Marxists had found little or no evidence to convict the Thulist prisoners, so false charges were created to incriminate them.

The Bavarian Soviet Republic, which was already on the point of economic and social collapse, sealed their own annihilation with this act. Although the Red Guards numbered 20,000 armed militia, most of them only signed up in order to get food to feed their starving families, and as soon as the writing was on the wall, many threw away their red armbands and deserted. Others left due to the 'foreignness' of the ring leaders who proclaimed an obvious hatred for the Bavarian working and middle classes that the same Marxist pseudo-intellectual leadership were claiming to represent. The murder of the Thule prisoners was the final straw in what became a depraved and psychotic revolution with no clear objectives other than mayhem and oppression under a barbaric red flag. The Bavarian Soviet Republic had no high moral ground on which to win the support of the working classes living in Munich and other cities within southern Germany.

Some deserted and ran to the advancing Thule Combat League troops, who were clearing out the suburbs on their way to the city centre announcing to the invasion force that 'the Reds' had executed

Thule prisoners, and had also raped the female prisoners and the genitalia had been cut off the male prisoners. Although these allegations of sexual mutilation turned out to be untrue, hearing them only increased the determination of the Prussian *Freikorps* and Thule Combat League to launch an all-out attack on the Bavarian Soviet Republic within Munich city centre in which Rudolf Hess would be injured attacking a Red Guard machine gun position. The remaining Red Guards who continued to fight were overwhelmed by the tactics and bravery of the *Freikorps* and Thule Combat League, who seemed fearless in the face of flying bullets, and took surprisingly few casualties, considering the intensity of the fighting on the streets of Munich. Their no-nonsense tactics and stoicism in the face of death impressed ordinary citizens who watched them march casually into barricades manned by Red Guard troops and easily overwhelmed them. Within their ranks were images of the Skull and Crossbones, along with a strange double '*SS*' runic design on their equipment and uniforms, and most intriguing of all, that broken cross symbol. They marched into Munich and crushed the Marxists similar to crusaders liberating the Holy Land. They had more than politics driving them; they had a spiritual war plan to recapture the city.

At the same time that Lenin was proclaiming in Moscow that May Day 1919 was to celebrate the establishment of the new Bavarian Soviet Republic, the Red Guards—and anyone else who was suspected of being a member of the Spartacist League—were treated without mercy. Max Levien, the fanatical Bolshevik, who bore a huge responsibility for the blood bath of revenge killings sparked by his fanaticism and stupidity, sneaked weasel-like out of the city under the cover of darkness eventually to make his way back to Russia via Austria. He left his 'comrades' behind to be beaten, tortured and murdered as a direct consequence of his appalling and vicious fanatical actions.

The ruthless carnage in the aftermath of the crushing of the Bavarian Soviet Republic unleashed a dark spell of brutality which was to be later brought into industrial-level fruition by the *SS*. The first mass killing involving a religious group during this Black-Häxan-Pagan revival took place at The Society of Saint Joseph meeting, where twenty one Catholic workers who were in the parish hall rehearsing for a pageant play were beaten and stabbed to death by members of the Prussian Guards Cavalry. Even Christians were not safe from the new jack-booted marching Teutonic war gods of Germany. Munich was a very different place now, and in time, from the events of *Walpurgis Night/May Day* 1919, Germany and the world would never be the same again.

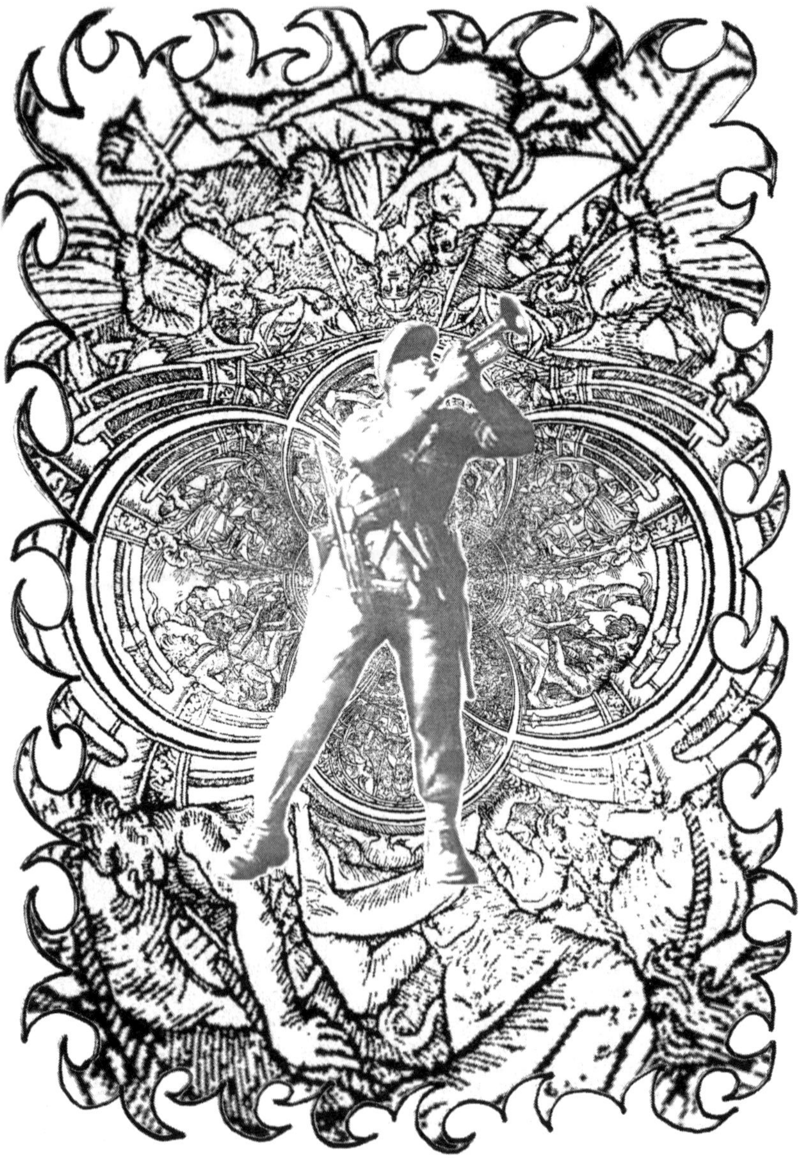

SEVEN

THE WITCH'S HAMMER

"Terror made me cruel . . ."

— Emily Brontë

No sooner had the fighting ceased and the Thule Society had risen to the level of a major influential force within Germany, than the news came through of the death of Guido von List in Berlin from a lung inflammation. The highly influential 19th century occultist who popularised the veneration of Druidic and Nordic pagan deities within a popular folk-spiritual movement developed as a counterpoint to the rapid industrialisation of central and western Germany. Along with Lanz von Leibenfels, von List was a prolific producer and disseminator of occult and anti-Semitic literature. The underlying concept being that the spiritual force and identity of races was contained via their blood, and that the

German blood had been polluted and needed to be made clean again, were the primary influences on both the Thule Society and Adolf Hitler himself. The mystical racial-occult style of von List's pamphlets provided Adolf Hitler with a narrative of his own political ideology which he would later flesh out to the full extreme in his own grimoire *Mein Kampf*. Indeed, it is important for scholars of the present era to consider the pamphlets of von List and his Aryan racial identity propagandists of that time as more akin to magical spells designed to change the will of the German psyche.

Guido von List was also a member of Lanz von Leibenfels' Order of the Templars, where the 'Dark Ones' were decreed to be the enemy of the Aryan peoples. Nothing less than a racial Battle of Armageddon —according to Guido von List—would be required to release the Germans from their enslavement by inferior races. It was von List who formulated the concept and governmental structures of the Third Reich as what he termed "the visible embodiment of the divine Aryan law." The double '*SS*' symbol was derived from the Runes, and which von List declared was partially magically potent and must become the symbol of the new Reich. Eventually, Himmler would adopt von List's '*SS*' symbol while Hitler chose the swastika flag developed by von List's fellow occultist Lanz von Leibenfels. Troops from the Thule Combat League were already painting both symbols on their helmets during their march on Munich in 1919, to stress that all these events were derived from Black-Häxan-Paganism and politically, everything else was secondary.

The Thule Society was now up and operating again inside their district at the Four Seasons Hotel, and with this, Ritter von Epp was promoted to general for his leadership during the Munich siege, to take command of the *Reichswehr IV*. This new military force was comprised of the remnants of the Bavarian *Freikorps* and local army units stationed in the city. Ernst Röhm and Rudolf Hess were both officers under von Epp's command. The Four Seasons Hotel went from being used by the Thule Society for the purpose of conducting magical occult rituals to one of the most politically powerful nerve centres in central Europe.

The Thule Society now had a stage on which to spellbind the world. All that was needed now was a master magician with the will to unleash the full power of the swastika. While the cities of Germany had become battlegrounds for political and occultic ideologies, the German psyche was also locked in a state of battle, and the cultural manifestations of the times would provide an oracle into the tormented Teutonic consciousness from 1919 onward.

THE SIGIL OF THOR ROTATES FULL CIRCLE

A few weeks after the death of Guido von List, members of the Thule Society conducted a seance inside the Four Seasons Hotel, involving a Russian female peasant who—if reports are to believed—manifested the spiritual forms of the murdered Prince von Thurn und Taxis and Countess von Westarp. To the terrified and amazed attendees, the ghosts of the murdered Thule Society aristocrats announced the imminent arrival of the German Messiah who had been longed for all these dark years.

The dialect in which the spirits allegedly spoke was the 'Low German' (*Plattdeutsch*), derived from the ancient *Old Saxon* tongue. However, the apparitions also came with a dire warning that this Messiah would be a false prophet who would lead Germany into destruction. The two apparitions vanished from sight—and this is highly significant—the attending delegation ignored the portents of doom. This event also raises the possibility of the spiritual apparitions of the murdered Prince von Thurn und Taxis and Countess von Westarp being what Islamic and other esoteric traditions would term as 'imposter Djinn'—or trickster demons—in that they were actually non-human entities pretending to be the ghosts of the prince and countess which were generated as tulpas (Tibetan manifested thought forms) in the minds of the attendees in order to trick them into causing chaos within the material world. We will simply never know the real truth of these events. Rather, we can only bear withness to the historical shadow they have cast across the last century.

FROM THE SOMNAMBULIST TO THE VAMPIRE

All societies have their mythology and their own living myths. Myth is not a product of the past. Myth reflects the subconscious dynamics of the society from which the mythology manifests. Such myth is not passive. It is highly reactive to the collective consciousness of the population who are both generating and being subjected to the archetypes and hidden narratives contained within the specific story or archetypes. In Germany, from the end of the Great War and into the formative years of National Socialism, the cinema, more than any other form of popular entertainment, reflected the turbulence of the Germanic soul in a series of very popular silent horror movies which were presented on the big screen; the monsters which were waiting to be reborn within the subconscious of the Germanic post-Great War psyche.

One cannot view the social and political context of the early years of the Weimar Republic in purely cold, socio-economic terms. Humans possess a far greater degree of emotional and psychological complexity than how they are told to feel about unemployment percentages, the rate of inflation, or the cost of bread. We can look at the economic data and political realities of that time and it will tell us practically nothing concerning how the people of Germany felt emotionally, or even spiritually, in the wake of their national catastrophe and the turmoil which was continually unfolding around them at the time.

For this, we have to look much deeper by means of examining the culture, and in particular, the popular culture of Germany in and around the year 1919. For this, the cinema provides the most accessible oracle. The production, themes and popularity (at the box office) of films primed the German subconscious for what was to come, and which would release the dark ghosts of the Teutonic psyche once again. By reading into the narrative and archetypes of these films, we can see a culture reacting to a kind of esoteric pornography. Narratives aimed not at their libido, but at their primal core of a suppressed shadow self-identity—on the verge of exploding in frustration and repressed anger—by the plots and messages contained within these films, to light the fuse of their psyche illuminating what was really going on within the psychology of the society at that time. A fuse which would eventually explode out of the hidden Black-Häxan-Paganism desires, fears and inclinations from below the surface and surrender them to Adolf Hitler and the

Third Reich.

THE CABINET OF DOCTOR CALIGARI (1919)

Easily among the greatest masterpieces of world cinema and one which never ceases to amaze and intrigue the viewer, for no other reason than we are seeing the psychic condition of a nation at the time of the film's production and release. A film which was to go on to be considered an oracle of the Germanic mythos during 1919 and beyond. The story begins in a small hamlet near the Dutch border, in which a fairground sideshow by a Dr. Caligari arrives along with his somnambulist (a sleepwalking seer) named Cesare. During the night, Cesare, wearing only a black body stocking and with a ghostly white face, slithers through the distorted streetscapes murdering anyone Dr. Caligari orders him to kill.

After his friend has been found dead, a young student named Francis takes a suspicious interest in Dr. Caligari. This results in Cesare being sent out to murder Francis' fiancée Joan. Upon catching sight of Joan, the somnambulist is captivated by her beauty and decides to abduct her instead. The abduction, however, is in vain, as Cesare collapses from exhaustion and dies. Dr. Caligari is identified as the controlling agent of the somnambulist Cesare and then, in a brilliant twist in the plot, turns out to be a director of an insane asylum who, when confronted by the corpse of Cesare, goes mad. The entire story is told from the perspective of the student Francis.

The plot was written by Carl Mayer and the production was undertaken in collusion with the expressionist art group *Der Sturm* from Berlin. The style and look of the film was completely unique, nightmarish and strikingly powerful at the time of original cinema release, and still remains so to modern viewers. Buildings and scenery are set at irregular angles and perspectives; the movements of Cesare (played by Werner Krauss) are lingeringly disturbing, as if portraying the play of his own shadow upon the backdrop, rather than himself being in the foreground.

As is the case with the artistic creative muse—when it captures an individual or group—the nature of the creative intention tends to transport the artist(s) outside the current paradigm, and this can have consequences beyond the artist's original intention, getting carried away in the creative originality, while failing to comprehend the effects which the aesthetic originality may be having upon the society viewing the completed artwork. In the case of *The Cabinet of Dr. Caligari*, I feel that this social knock-on effect was no mere accident of the project, nor even the short-sightedness of the film's creators. It was *meant to happen* as it did, when it did.

As the Great War had just ended, the film was indirectly stating to the German viewer that their leaders were insane and they were the ones who made somnambulists of all Germans, and then sleepwalked their fathers, brothers and sons into the meat grinders of Verdun and the Somme. This message rang loud and clear with the millions of disillusioned Germans who nervously watched the movie in the darkened cinemas. Authority itself was 'insane', and the Weimar Republic, created by the Treaty of Versailles, was an insane asylum created as punishment for the Germans.

The original release prints of the film were hand-tinted in green, brown and cold blue hues which would have impacted the narrative upon the viewers' consciousness to a far greater degree than ordinary black and white would have. With the rise of Adolf Hitler and the Third Reich, this overtone of the Weimar Asylum only became more resonant, in that *The Cabinet of Dr. Caligari* was the initial spark which lit the fuse of the need for some form of Germanic salvation from the national asylum. All this was taking place at the same time that Adolf Hitler was undergoing a series of psychedelic experiences while he was recovering in a military hospital from his injuries from the Great War.

DER GOLEM (1920)

The Jews, although perpetually looked upon as outsiders—even when they attempted to fully integrate and be accepted as "Germans"—were a community which had a very old history living in Germany that went right back to antiquity. In 1920, a movie was released which became a major success in Germany, and which accidentally infused in Germans the idea that Jews were not only very different to Germans, but had something which Germany had long lost: supernatural powers. *Der Golem, Wie er in die Welt kam (The Golem: How He Came Into the World)* was a silent horror film starring Paul Wegener with a script adapted from the 1915 novel by Gustav Meyrink. Paul Wegener had originally played the role in 1914, but was unhappy with the original production and script. In order to play the role once again, and have the story adhere more with the legend as it was told to him while he was working in Prague the previous year, Wegener brought in Carl Boese as his co-director and hired screen writer Henrik Galeen to flesh out Wegener's recounting of the tale.

Based on actual events which took place in the Bohemian capital under the reign of Holy Roman Emperor Rudolf II, it surrounds an actual historical figure—the famous Jewish scholar named Rabbi Loew—and a clay monster which he created and brought to life using the Jewish magical system of Kaballah. The story begins with a dream-like scene showing Rabbi Loew, who is also the head of the Jewish ghetto, observing astronomical objects while consulting astrology charts which he determines predicts destruction for the Jews of Prague. Soon after, the Holy Roman Emperor signs a royal decree stating that the Jews must leave within a month.

An effeminate Christian knight named Florian is dispatched to deliver the decree to Rabbi Loew. The self-impressed and flamboyant Florian finds himself smitten with Loew's daughter Miriam, while Rabbi Loew implements a plan to save his people of expulsion from the city. Rabbi Loew begins to create—according to the instructions within a Kabbalistic text—a giant human-shaped monster made from clay. During one of the most esoteric and occult sequences ever committed to film, the Rabbi performs a magical ceremony in order to bring the clay monster to life so as to impress the Emperor and win his favour, thereby saving his community.

Der Golem is a stunningly visual film, nearly a full century since its release. The sense of 'otherworldliness' of the Jewish ghetto only reinforces the supernatural quality of life within the Jewish community. The buildings are more akin to *Expressionist* mountains with the Jews living inside portrayed more like non-human alien beings than humans; aliens beings with mysterious and magical powers.

The film has no anti-Semitic agenda or narrative, as the Prague ghetto Jews are clearly portrayed as politically powerless and impoverished. The 'differences' of the Jews from the Gentiles they lived amongst would not have been lost on Germans watching it at the time. Especially in Munich, where only a year before German occultists had defeated mostly Jewish revolutionaries. The Munich right-wing press constantly drummed-up references to 'Jewish-Reds', while recounting their atrocities during the Bavarian Soviet Republic, conveniently omitting that not all the Reds were Jews, and some of their victims were well-liked and respectable middle class Jewish professionals and business people.

However, within the accidental sub-plot of *Der Golem*, the message is clear: even when the Jews are poor and broken, they still possess great magical abilities that the Gentiles are at the mercy of. The local Christians in the film are portrayed as pasty-faced secular innocents, especially when things go wrong and the Golem is taken over by the Rabbi's jealous assistant Famulus. At that time, Germans who were racially minded would have used the story of the film to underpin their beliefs that Jews are potentially dangerous and very alien. Religious and rural Germans would have been disturbed by the convincing imagery of sorcery in the film, which can be easily stereotyped as 'black magic' in the eyes of a devout Christian, and extrapolate this to imply that the Jewish religion is a form of devil worship, and further, that the movie ends with a large *Star of David* appearing magically on the cinema screen. One can only imagine the satisfaction the Thule Society took from this movie as it essentially justified their own Black-Häxan-Pagan revival to protect Germans from 'Jewish magic'.

Deutschlands Befreiung

EIGHT

PANZER OF THE PSYCHE

"(Hitler's) speeches are the day dreams of the mass soul..."

— Konrad Heiden

Following his recovery from injuries as a decorated, front-line soldier in the Great War, Adolf Hitler arrived in the Bavarian city of Munich unemployed and searching for a stage on which to perform his craft. Deeply resentful of Germany's treatment and humiliation at the Versailles conference, he became an army spy and an infiltrator within the German Workers' Party (DAP), more out of something to keep him occupied than any personal distrust he had of the organisation. Prior to this, Hitler appeared to be somewhat politically flexible, having not yet nailed his colours to any specific ideological mast. Justice for Germany—from either side —was Hitler's only agenda. His main brief as an infiltrator was to influence former ex-military men who were being recruited by the party and to steer them away from joining up, as the military discouraged all political activism among professional soldiers.

Even if he had yet to fully commit himself to any political party, it was during this time that Hitler found himself drawn to the speeches of DAP founder Anton Drexler. What Drexler provided Hitler with were not new ideas, but a political and social framework on which he could neatly copper-fasten his own convictions and prejudices. Convictions and prejudices which were to allow the future Führer to set the political and esoteric roadmap for the rest of his life. 1919 was the year Adolf Hitler was activated to the full extent of what he could potentially deliver.

The die was rapidly becoming cast. Hitler acquired one of Drexler's pamphlets entitled *My Political Awakening*, in which the author outlined his racial theories and how they related to the current Germanic predicament. Hitler was later to call this turning point—and many others like it—the point where the 'Goddess of Fate' (Ostara) intervened. Hitler read the booklet with frantic excitement, as it revealed to him a political manifesto on which he could overlay his occult beliefs. Drexler, it just so happened, was also a gun-running member of the Thule Society.

ACTIVATION AND AGENCY

Prior to his encounter with Drexler and the Thule Society, Adolf Hitler was remarkable in how unremarkable he was. People who knew him growing up, and during his time in the army, noted nothing special or powerfully charismatic about him. He was just another face in the crowd. Apart from his ability to paint landscapes with a high degree of proficiency in watercolours, the only other aspect that made him stand out was his interest in the operas of Wagner and the occult. In particular, the occult history of Germany, in which Hitler was indeed something of an expert. By the time the Thule Society had encountered Adolf Hitler, they numbered almost 2,000 members conducting occult rituals, running guns, producing vast amounts of propaganda and organising attacks on Reds. Although it appears that Hitler was not a member of the Thule Society, he was "often a guest", and made regular visits to the Four Seasons Hotel, where it becomes highly plausible that during these visits, he received his magical training, including his ability to mesmerise people with his intense eyes.

FASCINATION

Hitler had one aspect of his being that everyone who had ever encountered him personally from 1919 onwards constantly remarked about: his eyes, and their ability to penetrate to the core of anyone who looked into them. Like helpless prey frozen in the stare of a cobra, people would be captivated, left powerless and mesmerised after staring into Hitler's eyes. Childhood friends had told how, as a youngster, the blue colour of his eyes, while being beautiful in colour and vibrancy, were not necessarily hypnotic. Hitler's eyes were noted more for their appearance than their powers. The only place he could have developed the abilities to mesmerise people with his eyes was via his association with the Thule Society during the summer months of 1919, as one of their guests. One of the occultists within the Thulist circle (possibly Rudolf Hess) must have noticed the highly exceptional eyes of Adolf Hitler, and then indoctrinated him in the skill of Eye Magic (or *Fascination*) in order to use his stare to captivate people to the astounding levels he was later capable of achieving.

Fascination is the ability of a witch or occultist to use their stare in order to 'reach the heart' of their target, and therefore place them under the will of the occultist's Eye Magic. The belief is that the blood vessels in the eyes of a person are easily accessed in terms of placing the life force of the magician into the blood in the eyes of the person they wish to control. This 'bewitched' blood (which, in Teutonic occultism, the life force of blood is the basis of all spiritual forces) within the eyes is then pumped to the heart, resulting in the target being under the influence of *Fascination*. Rasputin was another powerful occultist who had this ability to control others with his eyes, and, if done correctly, *Fascination* can infect the behaviour of the beholder similar to a disease which they have no immunity from. Titus Lucretius Carus, a Roman poet and philosopher, wrote of the effects of *Fascination*:

> *The body smitten is, but yet the mind*
> *Is wounded with the darts of Cupid blind.*
> *All parts do Sympathize i' th' wound, but know*
> *The blood appears in that which had the blow.*

The German stage actor Gerhart Hauptmann, upon staring into Adolf Hitler's eyes for the first time, later recalled it as the greatest moment of his life, while the daughter of the US Ambassador to Germany, Martha Dodd, stated that looking into Adolf Hitler's eyes was "startling and unforgettable..." Hitler was known to have practised staring at his own eyes into mirrors before meeting with important dignitaries in order to disarm them with his hypnotic and penetrating gaze. Therese Förster-Nietzsche, sister of the famous philosopher, stated that she was both impressed and terrified of Hitler's stare. "They...searched me through and through."

THE GUEST OF THE NATION

During the summer of 1919, Adolf Hitler, now age 30, began to develop his oratory skills and his ability to captivate an audience, something he showed no proficiency in prior to his time as a guest of the Thule Society at the Four Seasons Hotel. At the military base at Augsburg, many of the troops stationed there were soon captivated by Hitler's speeches. Among them was Hans Knoden, who recalled that Hitler was suddenly and inexplicably developing into a brilliant and gifted speaker, and that eager listeners at the camp were signing up for his regular lectures.

At this time, Hitler was also working as a spy for the army who were using servicemen to monitor various political meetings around the city. It was almost as if Hitler had been brought out of his shell just by being in contact with the Thule Society, and by summer 1919, was being 'tested' to see if he had what the Thule Society needed from him: the potential to be the '*Fraja-Christus*': the Aryan Jesus of the resurrected Germany.

One of the groups whose meetings and activities the military developed an interest in were the German Workers Party, which had been founded in early 1919 by a locksmith named Anton Drexler and his associate, a journalist named Karl Harrer. The group decided early on in the formation that anti-Bolshevik and anti-Jewish pro-working class agenda was the key to developing an influential nationalist movement within Bavaria, based on the ideology of the Fatherland Party and the German Nationalist Protection and Defiance Federation (*Deutschvölkischer Schutz und Trutzbund*). All these groups were in communication with the Thule Society, which tended to be more middle-class and bohemian in terms of membership.

On September 11, 1919, Adolf Hitler was told of a meeting to be held the following night, hosted by the Thule Society inside a pub on the Tal in central Munich, which he was to infiltrate on behalf of his Bavarian regiment. What took place was nothing less than the metamorphism of Adolf Hitler into the future Black-Häxan-Pagan witch king of the Third Reich. Hitler entered the tavern on the following night and listened to a proposal for the creation of an independent Bavaria, delivered by an individual named Professor Baumann. Hitler rose to his feet and delivered a rebuttal against the break up of Germany that impressed all who were present.

By the end of the month, Hitler turned his back on his regiment and joined the German Workers Party, which were to become the Nazis in the course of time. He was given the membership number 555 and his committee number was 7. In numerology, 555 signifies turbulent changes are coming to pass, while the number 7 is a highly significant number at the centre of all mystical traditions across the globe. It is the number of stellar objects in the solar system visible to the naked eye from Earth: the Sun, the Moon and the five classical naked eye planets: Mars, Mercury, Jupiter, Venus and Saturn. There are seven chakras in the Vedic tradition (from which the swastika originates), seven days of the week, and so on. The German Workers Party, under the possible direction of the Thule Society, would have presented Hitler with these specific numbers, hardly ignorant of their numerological significance. Likewise, Hitler would have also understood their significance to the same degree.

SCORES TO BE SETTLED

Before Hitler went to Munich, he had already read the anti-Semitic works of Lanz von Leibenfels, Guido von List, Richard Wagner and H.S. Chamberlain. The racial aspect of the Thule Society's agenda would have been very familiar to him. However, this time it came with a chance of real political opportunity. Hitler had come a long way from the time he lived in Vienna back in 1909, reading copies of the esoteric newsletter *Ostara*. It is indeed remarkable to think that during Hitler's birth and formative years, Germany was being culturally ingrained with a need for a magical Führer to liberate the nation from democracy and racial contamination. This was the sense of destiny that both Adolf Hitler and his supporters viewed as the script that he would, and must follow.

Hitler, in many regards, was an actor who was born for a leading performance that had been scripted in the years before and up to his birth. Two 19th century writers were responsible for this sense of a Teutonic Messiah that was needed to liberate the German soul: Paul Anton de Lagarde (1827-91) and Julius Langbehn (1851-1907). The ideas and beliefs they both unleashed upon the Germanic consciousness were merely waiting for the right person to fill the role.

During his lifetime, Paul Anton de Lagarde created an enormous body of work, and whom Thomas Mann—the 1929 Nobel Laureate—referred to as one of the giants of German culture. Indeed, de Lagarde's stature was held in the same high esteem as Nietzsche and Wagner up until the end of the Second World War. His most influential work was the mystical book, *Deutsche Schriften* (*German Writings*), published in 1878, which made de Lagarde a household name in the German-speaking world. Disgusted by democracy and emerging liberalism, his statement "demoracy and culture are mutually exclusive" was a popular slogan during the early days of the Nazi Party in Munich. In terms of his political writings, de Lagarde called for the creation of a new German empire of racially clean Germans. The 'volk' were to be freed from the liberalising influence of the urban Jews and bohemian pseudo-intellectuals, and this liberation would result in a new *Renaissance* of Teutonic cultural and spiritual restoration; a kind of exorcism for the German blood. Just over a decade before Adolf Hitler was born, this situation could only be attained, de Lagarde argued, with the arrival of a new mystical and magical Führer riding on the crest of nationalism and racial purity.

In his hugely popular book *Rembrandt als Erzieher* (*Rembrandt as Educator*), the art historian Julius Langbehn proposed that the Dutch painter Rembrandt van Rijn was a mystic of racist nationalism. The book, published in 1890, claimed that Rembrandt was an example of a Germanic artist polluted by racial intermixing, and amazingly, the book was held in high regard by many German intellectuals of the era. Wilhelm von Bode, the curator of the Prussian art collections in Berlin, praised the book's representation of the German spirit, while Karl Ernst Osthaus, the future founder of the *Museum Folkwang*, cited Langbehn as being one of his major influences.

In what could have been one of the most pivotal cultural turning points—if not one of the great tragedies—of cultural bastardisation, Langbehn unsuccessfully tried to convince Friedrich Nietzsche's family to hand over sole control of Nietzsche's work to him in order to finance a 'cure' for the philosopher's mental predicaments.

Langbehn then went on to distort Nietzsche's writings (as did the Third Reich in time), and this resulted in *Rembrandt als Erzieher* being continually praised by the Nazis leading up to, and all during the Second World War. In many ways, Langbehn can be considered the cultural stepping stone between Richard Wagner and the creation of Adolf Hitler; he made racist ideology and anti-Semitism 'respectable' among millions of Germans in a manner which Wagner's own racial writings were unable to manage. One of Landbehn's most powerful and ominous statements was his call for a new Barbarossa to lead Germany with an "artistic temperament...a Kaiser Artist...whose fire of...spirit and strength of arm will fulfil our ancient victorious longings."

THE ROMANTIC GHOSTS OF THE GERMANIC HEART

Adolf Hitler began his career as a magician while still in his teens, following what can only be looked upon in hindsight as a psychedelic or shamanic experience during a performance of Wagner's opera, entitled *Rienzi, der Letzte der Tribunen (WWV 49)* or in English, *Rienzi, the Last of the Tribunes*. Aware of his own psychological need (perhaps due to the appalling father figure he had as a child) to become a central figure in the course of human destiny, the young Adolf Hitler viewed the opera as a narrative for his own desire for greatness and personal heroism. Saturated in mystical coagulation of Germanic myth and magic, Wagner's opera had such an intoxicating effect on the young Hitler that he almost immediately began to frantically study Germanic mythology, magic and the occult.

Incredible as it seems, by the second decade of the 20th century, the 'new Barbarossa' was already building his empire in the pubs of Munich, tailor-made to slot into the archetype created in the minds of de Lagarde and Langbehn. It was akin to two writers creating manifestos about the need for the arrival of an anti-Christ, and within a couple of decades the Anti-Christ arrives, which proves the point I have always made: that artists and 'their craft' have a far greater responsibility to humanity than they are often aware of. The old adage can be applied to the German racist artists of the 19th century: be careful what you imagine, because sometimes your magic will come into reality. In the case of de Lagarde, Langbehn and Richard Wagner, they manifested Adolf Hitler from their misguided and racist creative intentions.

PHILOSOPHY AND IDENTITY

Hitler's power as an orator was that he delivered startling rhetorical performances which were both intimidating and intriguing to the listener. To many he looked fanatical, and indeed this was done on purpose, as a fiery delivery made with pleading hands and pounding fists, if nothing else, caught the attention of people in Munich, and once they were in the door, then they could be influenced.

The charismatic evangelical overtones issued by Adolf Hitler called upon German manhood to take up their weapons, and by the early 1920s, people were already comparing Adolf Hitler to Martin Luther. Hitler was also unique in Bavaria; no other speaker had his ability to captivate and spellbind an audience. That is because no other political speaker in Bavaria was a trained magician.

THE WORD PLAYS

Another example of academics failing to understand how Adolf Hitler operated and worked people is their inability to understand Hitler's speeches and performances at public rallies. All of Hitler's techniques, from the arm waving to the long pauses to the purposeful delaying—all the while generating a sense of prolonged expectation—are all rooted in occult rituals. They were not simply the eccentric manifestations of a madman. These practised and rehearsed techniques were all designed to focus Hitler's will into the consciousness of the listener. The silence between the sentences and the race towards the crescendo at the very end were all hypnotic elements derived from ritual magic.

Hitler's early speeches are often cited by historians as proof that he was not the great orator that some believe him to have been, and that his bombastic delivery at the very start of his addresses suggests that he was unstable and not in control of his faculties. They claim that Hitler was just ranting because he could not control himself. Nothing could be further from the truth. Adolf Hitler was completely in control during every speech he ever gave. The opening bombastic and divisive salvo of accusations and incriminations at the start of his early speeches was to rout out hidden enemies and beligerents within the crowd by causing them to become angry and thus reveal themselves. Then they could be beaten up and ejected from the meeting, after which the 'real' meeting could then begin.

This initial exposing of infiltrators at meetings would also foster a sense of bonding between Adolf Hitler and the crowd at the early events. He was not there just to deliver a speech, but they were also in his hands while he was in charge. Brilliantly manipulative, it has to be said, and a spell which would have been very powerful in a violent and aggressive city such as Munich in the early 1920s. Again, this is another technique derived from occult rituals, where an initiate is subjected to trauma and abuse, and even assaults, in order to see if they are serious about their intent to join the sect or cult. Adolf Hitler was building a religion after all, and not just a political organisation.

Adolf Hitler knew precisely what he was doing and why he was doing it. He had spent decades reading and studying occult subjects and rituals, and through his involvement as a 'guest' with the Thule Society, his ability to finally and fully utilise these occult techniques began to bear fruit almost instantly. The crowds were starting to build, as more and more people flocked to his speeches. Not only the working class and the unemployed, but also engineers, doctors and scientists who were often impressed by the range of subject matter he covered, along with Hitler's current knowledge concerning the latest technical and scientific innovations.

Hitler's occult training was implemented within the dynamics of his early lectures in order to create an emotional bond with the audience; to enchant and control their perceptions, thus generating a magical sense of anticipation and drama. Following the initial bombastic assault on his enemies, Hitler would then deliver a depressing and hopeless summary of the condition of Germany at that time. Comparing Germany to that of a colony (which was not entirely untrue), he would move the energetic dynamics of the speech towards inciting anger and frustration amongst the crowd. Then, he would inform them that they were a nation of victims, but that this was not of their doing. This was implemented by Hitler in order to move the psychological goalposts of the audience towards them needing salvation; finally ending in a bombastic and fiery culmination of liberation and the honour of Germany restored. The effect these speeches had on audiences who listened to them were often intoxicating, and soon people were travelling from around Bavaria to listen to Hitler's speeches.

WITNESS TO MAGIC

Hans Frank, who was later to become the leader of Poland under the Nazis, first heard Hitler speak in January 1920, and noted that although he was indeed bombastic and "intense like a fanatic", Hitler conveyed a sense of sincere honesty to the crowd, in that he was not trying to sell them an idea he himself did not fully believe in. Hitler's conviction was driven home by the dramatic pauses, as he would push back his hair and the passionate intensity of his blue eyes made direct contact with everyone in the room. Hans Frank felt as if "his heart struck a chord with every word Hitler uttered" as he shone a light out of the grim gutter of post-Great War Germany and towards a new tomorrow, addressed in a very personal way to all who were present. All methods of hypnosis, *Fascination* and enchantment techniques were derived from the occult arts. In the autumn of 1922, Hermann Göring went to listen to Hitler giving an address on the crimes of the Versailles Treaty, to which Göring declared soon after, "The conviction was spoken word for word as if from my own soul." Later, the British Ambassador to Germany, Sir Neville Henderson, would write, "He (Hitler) owed his success in the struggle for power to the fact that he was the reflection of their (party members) subconscious mind, and his ability to express in words what the subconscious mind felt that it wanted." It mattered not that the political ideas delivered by Adolf Hitler were simplistic and unsophisticated. His conviction magic aimed for the hearts of his followers, first and foremost. His speeches were, in actuality, spiritual outpourings of the broken German soul, and any complex political ideas were irrelevant in the context of these sermons.

Although Adolf Hitler was essentially delivering a restoration of pagan religious ideals carefully hidden inside political manifestos, he had to be careful not to alienate Catholics in Bavaria at that time. As late as April 1922, Hitler was still making references to Jesus Christ in the context of a fighter who had been betrayed by Judas (Jews), and that it was up to good men to defend themselves from the Judas within Germany. There would be mentions of the 'vipers' in the Temple (Germany) and the scourge of 'adders' which Jesus expelled. All very clever uses of word play and an early form of Neuro-Linguistic Programming (NLP). Later on, in typical cult leader fashion, Hitler and the Nazis would validate these early speeches by declaring that Jesus wasn't Jewish according to National Socialism; that he was, in fact, Aryan.

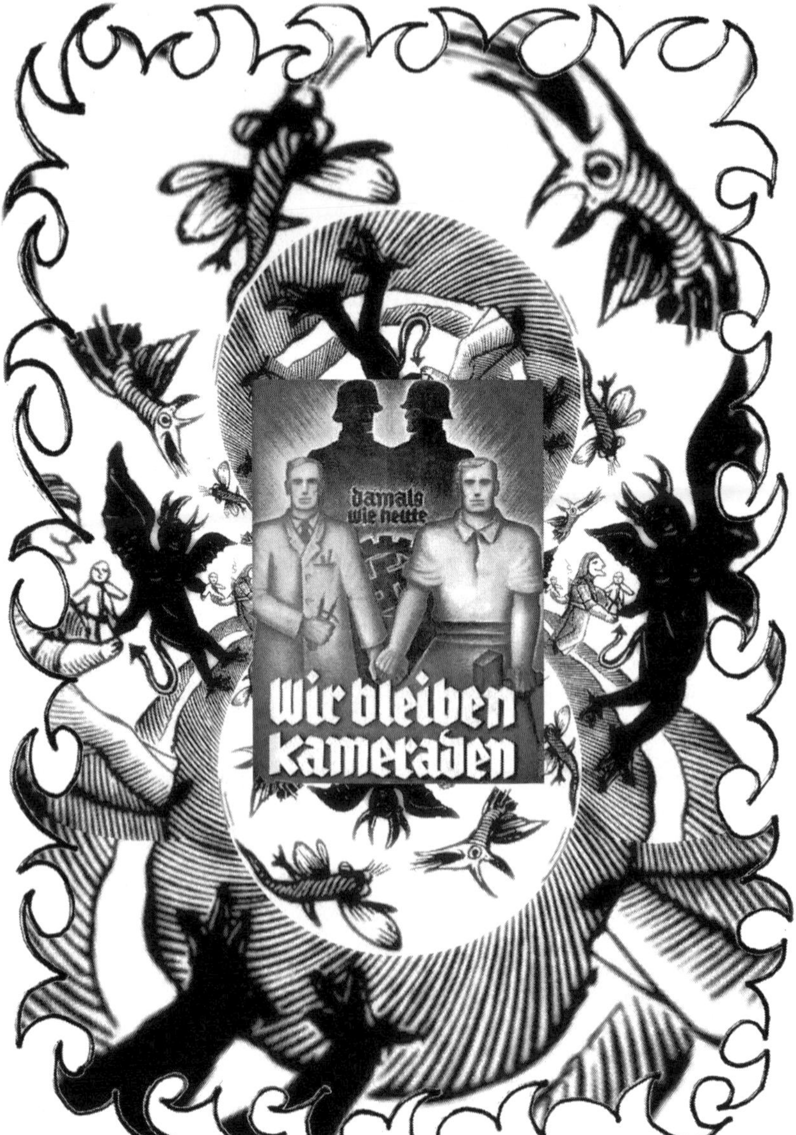
damals wie heute
Wir bleiben kameraden

NINE

TO BEHOLD AND BEWARE

"Whoever fights monsters should see to it that in the process he does not become a monster. And if you gaze long enough into an abyss, the abyss will gaze back into you."

— Friedrich Nietzsche

From my previous study into the subject of psychopathology, I have often been asked if psychopaths have souls. This is an impossible question to answer, although it is best approached that, if by 'soul' one means compassion and considerate empathy for other human beings, then the answer to this question would have to be no. Yet, so many psychopaths claim to have spiritual authority and set themselves up as leaders of churches, cults or invoke a spiritual dynamic to their personality in order to impress others. I firmly believe that psychopaths are unable to attain what most people might term a genuine 'spiritual experience', but they are still aware of the effects that 'spiritual experiences' have upon others. Similar to love and compassion, a spiritual experience to a psychopath is an alien concept, but much much the same as they do with love and compassion, they can fake it very well when targeting the audience they require.

One thing I am certain of is that psychopaths are capable of having what we have come to call a 'psychedelic' experience: this being a state of consciousness outside space and time, providing transformative experiences and insights. The psychedelic experience is very different than the spiritual experience, in that visions or revelations are present, while during a spiritual experience, even entire sensory perceptions can be muted and the 'state of grace' is still deeply experienced. Another aspect of the psychedelic experience is that while a normal person comes to feel the experience as an expression of connectedness and oneness with all humanity, nature and the cosmos, a psychopath undergoing a psychedelic experience tends to see it as proof that they themselves are either God, or have a special purpose or power which only they can deliver to the world.

Adolf Hitler, who seems to have devolved from proto-psychopath to full-blown psychopath during his rise to power (some would argue this was a result of on-going demonic possession), had several psychedelic experiences during his lifetime. In terms of his political fanaticism, the most significant experience appears to have taken place in November 1918, while he was recuperating in the army hospital at Pasewalk. For whatever reason, Hitler appears to have had a powerful psychedelic transformative visionary experience upon hearing the news that the German army had surrendered.

Later, many believed that Hitler was lying about the experience, and that he created a magical back story as part of his messiah myth. Certainly, the left-leaning *Munich Post* newspaper later on believed this to be the case—when Hitler became a public figure—but in this cynicism, their naïveté was also revealed. When cult leaders report having undergone a visionary experience, it is something to be taken very seriously indeed. If anything, Hitler had come to understand how powerful the supernatural transformative effect has upon most people, and he had learned how to trigger the same state of transformational change upon the German people, to place them under his own psychedelic transformative visionary power. Even if Hitler could not understand the music of the 'spiritual' experience, he was capable of reading—and far more importantly—writing the score.

SIGNS AND SYMBOLS

Incredible as it seems, within only a decade of Hitler's chance meeting with Dr. Walter Stein at the occult bookstore in Vienna, he would unleash, at the start of the fastest growing political movement at the time, the symbol of the swastika: the bent cross of National

Socialism, and one which, within another decade, was to fly over Europe stretching from The Hook of Holland all the way to the shores of the Black Sea. What was originally and still is a 'good luck' charm in the Vedic traditions of India—where it symbolised the life-giving rays of the Sun—became a black magic talisman for hundreds of millions who stood in its shadow. In Norse mythology, the swastika was identified as the Hammer of Thor in motion and, more fittingly, from the point of view of National Socialism, the *God of Thunder and Destruction*. Hitler again chose the National Socialist version of the swastika, based on the design flown by the Order of the Templars. Although on the surface, many of those close to Hitler during the early 1920s were not particularly taken by his esoteric beliefs, the fact remains that by this time, they would have been unknowingly enchanted and spellbound by his craft, completely oblivious to what magic actually is. Historians writing on the subject of Hitler's ability to have such an effect upon so many people at the time are seemingly unwilling or unable to make the connection between the 'magical' Hitler and the 'political' Hitler.

SIGNS OF THE TIME

At their very core, all cult leaders are psychopathic thugs with mysterious and cryptic associations, complex on-going criminality, diverse spiritual experimentation and contradictory personal histories behind the persona they present to their followers. This is the only persona that matters: the quasi-mystical leader who is somewhat flawed 'like the rest of us', but otherwise possessed with secret powers and a magical hidden knowledge which is used to hide the real knowledge of their actual seedy past. Adolf Hitler was no exception in this, and, just like any cult leader, in order for the new mythology of the saviour of Germany to be future-proofed and set in stone, the sins of the past had to be reengineered with a new back story.

Cult leaders do not just suddenly decide to become messianic figureheads at the helm of a group of deluded fanatics completely out of the blue one day. They were cult leaders long before they had a cult or a cult following, and they always behaved as if they were cult leaders even when they had only their own pathological reflection in the mirror following their every gesture and word. Psychopaths are known to use mirrors to fake the emotions and expressions which their targets require from them. The actual cult of devoted followers —when it arrives—eventually replaces the mirror, but performs precisely the same function.

The psycho-spiritual mirror of the cult followers comes to see the cult leader with the same sense of narcissistic adulation that the psychopathic cult leader observes, reflected back at them in their bathroom mirror. Hitler was no exception. Like all other psychopathic cult leaders, he had left a very messy trail of manipulated and discarded idealists, sadistic mind games played upon enablers and secret mayhem left in his wake. It would not have been possible for Adolf Hitler to have developed his craft without leaving such a legacy of devastation in his wake. Such is the stock and trade of all black magicians and cult leaders. Some flaunt their past devastation, while others with political or religious aspirations have to hide it. In order to become the Germanic messiah, Adolf Hitler had to first erase the demonic occult apprenticeship in his past. Then, he needed to annihilate all his past personas and with them, all who were aware of his pathological trajectory upon the world political stage.

AGENCY

As the 1920s commenced, Germans still longed for a hero to emerge with the strength to lead them to a new restored Fatherland. From 1923 onwards, Adolf Hitler was looking more and more to be that hero in eyes of thousands of Germans whom he had seduced with his speeches and conviction magic. The myth of the hero was never more important in Germany than after the Great War. Since the time of Bismark, who erected two hundred towers across Germany to celebrate the unification of the myriad of German states into a new nation, the German psyche longed for a knight to consolidate them emotionally and spiritually, similar to what Bismark had achieved politically. This aspect of the German psyche cannot be underestimated. At the time of Hitler's rise to leadership, one of the most popular tourist destinations was the *Hermann Monument* located in the Teutoburg Forest, commemorating the Germanic Cherusci chief Hermann, who in 9 AD destroyed the Roman legions commanded by Varus. The Teutonic psyche always seems to return to the forests and old woodlands to seek emotional and spiritual restoration. Especially in times of need. However, there are also monsters and demons lurking inside these woodlands masquerading as knights and angels ready to trap the gullible and the idealistic.

Prior to the Great War, members of the *Wandervogel* youth movement called for a new leader of Germany to rescue the nation from industrialisation and bring forth the return of rural and traditional culture. Inspired by Nietzsche, these youth revivalist groups were highly influential with large branches of membership, as well as smaller regional clubs all over Germany. Founded by Herman Hoffmann Folkersamb in 1901, the *Wandervogel* movement would later inspire the Hitler Youth movement, through bonding rituals around campfires, listening to stories of the Teutonic Knights and other Germanic heroic sagas. Championed by the likes of Richard Wagner, these movements were seen as a buffer against rapid liberalisation and commercial interests. The members of the *Wandervogel* and other rural spiritual movements who had survived the Great War would provide Adolf Hitler with a tailor-made audience, and in time, they would come to see him as the leader they yearned for in the recited songs they sang during their youthful campfire rituals.

THE COVEN

By 1923, Adolf Hitler and his conviction magic had brought Rudolf Hess, Hermann Göring, Heinrich Himmler, Joseph Goebbels, Alfred Rosenberg and nearly 16,000 other new members into the newly renamed National Socialists Workers Party. Another recruit, Ernst Röhm, had been particularly crucial to the growth and power of the party by creating their paramilitary wing known as the *Sturmabteilung* (*SA*) or Brownshirts, with an unmistakable Thule-inspired magical sigil as their emblem. The group was initially made up of former soldiers who acted, on a casual basis, as bouncers during early meetings, which mostly took place in pubs frequented by unemployed army men. Later on, recruitment into the National Socialists Workers Party would be further augmented by appealing to the urban unemployed and unskilled workers.

Part of the Brownshirt image was that they were forbidden to make speeches at events. The main purpose of the *SA* guards was to stand in silence and be ready to jump on anyone who caused trouble. They could not be reasoned with, spoken to, nor were they interested in what others—apart from their own side—had to say to them.

Already, the organisation was issuing statements that Hitler was the man who would rescue Germany, and this, coupled with their stoic aloofness, their magical insignia-adorned uniforms, flags and banners, would have been a very intimidating presence. The culture within the Brownshirts would have made them feel as if they were latter-day Vikings; fighting and then drinking beer afterwards to celebrate their victories. There was a dignity of sorts in these rituals, and dignity was a rare commodity for young German men at that time. Many young Germans joined the *SA* for practical purposes, as the uniform, and especially the boots, were a rarity at a time when clothing was very expensive. They were also paid an extra allowance on top of anything they received from the Labour Exchange when they went to sign on as unemployed. Hitler now had his own inner coven and the makings of a private army. The spells were coming to fruition at a rapid pace from 1922 onwards.

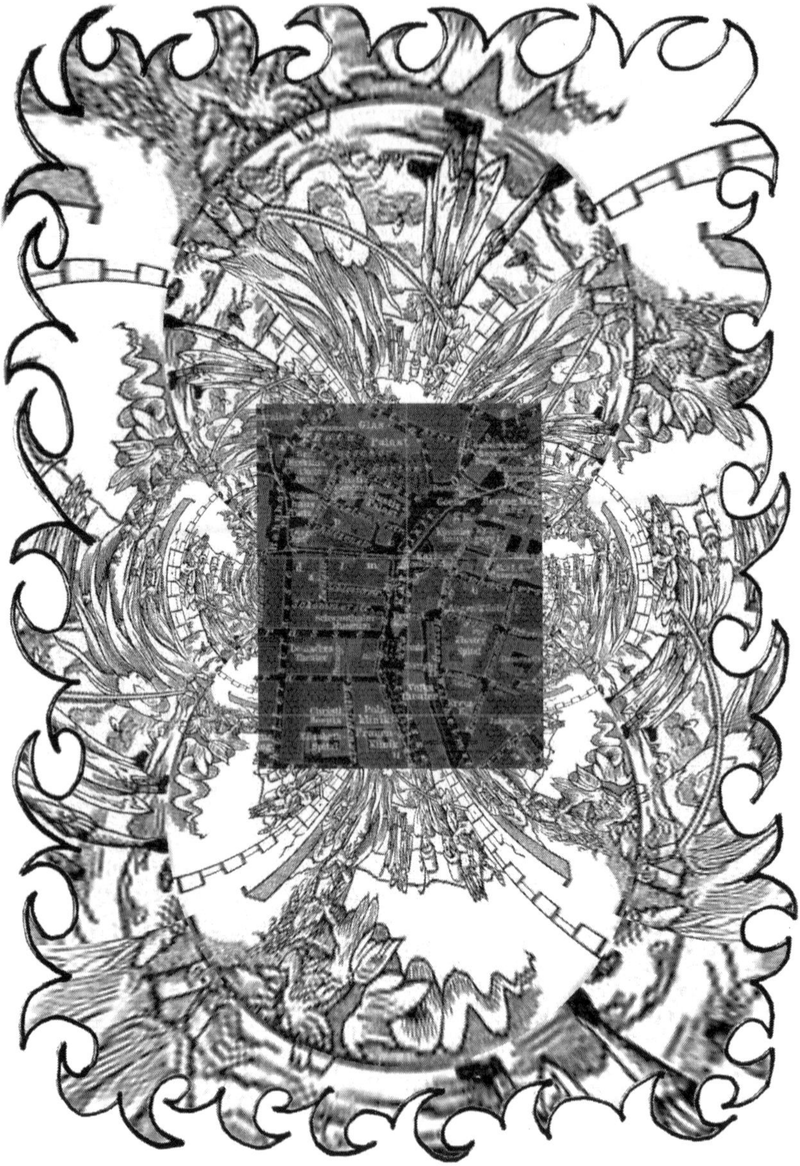

TEN

TRANSCENDENTAL MUNICH

"O, beware, my lord, of jealousy;It is the green-ey'd monster, which doth mock The meat it feeds on."

— William Shakespeare

Within days of the HOLLYWOOD sign being erected above the American movie magic capital, hyperinflation in Germany—which had increased two hundred times since the beginning of 1923—resulted in Germans requiring 353,000 Marks in order to purchase a single American dollar. However, elite Germans were getting very wealthy from dealing in scrap metal exports left over from the Great War due to the closing of factories and industries. While these profiteers existed in a culture of lavish indulgence and hedonistic lifestyles within the fashionable districts of Berlin, their decadence caused great resentment for many Germans living in destitution. This had been further compounded by military invasion of the Rhur by troops from France and Belgium in order to try and force Germany to make reparation payments to the mostly British and American banks who had given massive interest-laden loans to Germany under the guise of humanitarian aid; humanitarian aid to be paid back with crushing interest. The anger Germans felt at both the context and conditions of these loans was completely understandable at the time.

All these humiliating and soul-destroying factors coagulated to sicken and anger millions of ordinary Germans. Then the biggest bombshell occured: when on the September 26, the Bavarian State Commissioner, Gustav Ritter von Kahr declared Bavaria to be a sovereign state, no longer under the control of Berlin. With chaos ensuing in Saxony, and more uprising by the Marxists in Bavaria, at the time it must have seemed as if Germany was about to go the way of the Ottoman Empire and Austro-Hungary and vanish off the map forever, while the British, French, Belgian and Russian empires continued to carry on, with the United States ready to take their place of power once occupied by Germany.

An American empire had risen mainly due to Wall Street banks taking full advantage of the *1913 Federal Reserve Act,* allowing them to build and demolish nations at the stroke of a pen. Seizing the opportunity, the National Socialists were ready to become a major player on the political stage, and finally had hard political and social events to exploit for their own benefit. The next goal for Hitler and his party was to cultivate an emerging mythology to fuse their ideology, if not their heroic image, into the consciousness of the public at large. Adolf Hitler threw down the gauntlet, and demanded that the Bavarian government support the National Socialists on their march to Berlin to overthrow the 'criminals' in central government. This was a brazen act by a regional political party that was only four years in existence. The candle was moving ever closer to the powder keg.

Hitler and the Nazis were now embarking on their first large-scale ritual which would eventually give them the initiative they needed to force their will upon the entire German psyche. In other words, Hitler and the Nazis needed to follow the example of the Thule Combat League and fight and win—mainly on a psychological level —a very public battle. However, they needed to take it to the next level and fight in the open rather than from the relative seclusion of the Four Seasons Hotel. An epic of even greater magnitude than the 1919 'liberation' of Munich was needed in order for the '*Fraja-Christus*' living mythology of Adolf Hitler, the saviour of the German soul, to take root.

THE SHARDS OF SHATTERED GLASS

When people hear the phrase 'the Munich Beer Hall Putsch', images of a hapless Adolf Hitler—due mainly to how the event was portrayed in the Charlie Chaplin satirical film *The Great Dictator*—surrounded by fat drunken Germans flapping about in a disorganised farcical slapstick street fight generally comes to mind. This imagery still forms the basis of how most academic historians recall the events. It was nothing of the sort. The Munich Putsch on November 8-9, 1923 was a serious uprising which took real courage on behalf of the antagonists, and their bravery in the face of armed security forces left a deep impression upon the citizens of Munich. An impression that the hapless and vicious Marxist 'Spartacists revolutionaries and their terror squads lacked in 1919, as their Bolshevik leadership ran like rats from a sinking ship after they put the citizens of Munich through a living nightmare of oppression and random terror. The Munich Putsch of 1923 by Adolf Hitler and the National Socialists was far more gallant by comparison, and more importantly, the German people viewed it as such. Which was precisely the result the Thule Society, now pulling the strings via Rudolf Hess, their operative in the Nazi Party, desired.

A meeting had been arranged in Munich, at which the head of the Bavarian police and the commander of the German military would be present at the large Bürgerbräukeller hosted by the Bavarian State Commissioner Gustav von Kahr, who had implemented a state of martial law in order to deal with on-going street battles between Brownshirts and Marxist factions in the city centre. Inspired by Mussolini's *March on Rome*, Adolf Hitler entered the hall just after 8PM, along with Hermann Göring, Alfred Rosenberg, Rudolf Hess, and twenty five other senior party members, while six hundred heavily armed *SA*—including a machine gun crew—surrounded the beer hall. Hitler fired a shot from his revolver into the ceiling and jumped on a chair announcing: "The national revolution has broken out!".

Then, after casually ordering some beer, and without taking hostages or assaulting the dignitaries, Hitler discussed the situation with the attendees, and before the National Socialists left the meeting hall, they announced that a march on Munich would happen the next day, and proclaimed that if the revolution failed, then Hitler vowed to take his own life. He then ritualistically (to seal the pact) smashed his beer glass, which had some members of the crowd running to collect the broken fragments as if they were holy relics. This was epic theatrics in the extreme, and nothing less than a ritual designed to change the consciousness of all present in conformity with Hitler's will.

The entire event was a million miles away in terms of propaganda value than what Max Levien failed to achieve in 1919 issuing Marxist rhetoric while having innocent people shot in a school gymnasium. The National Socialist Munich Putsch of 1923 was specifically designed as a magic spell to undo the remaining sense of shame and lingering trauma left in the citizens of Munich by the horrors of the Spartacist Soviet four years previously. This was a ritual designed to *inspire* the Bavarians and the people of Munich, and not to intimidate them.

Hitler knew precisely what he was doing. But even so, the risks were incredibly high. However, the potential for success was even more powerful, depending on what would take place on November 9, the following day. Hitler, the Nazis, along with their Thule Society handlers in the shadows, had metaphorically pulled the *Death* card from the *Tarot* deck and presented it to all and sundry. It was going to either be the actual death of Hitler, or the death of the tortured Germanic consciousness. Adolf Hitler, for the first time, now had to stand completely outside the protection of the Thule Society's magic circle and demonstrate that he was as special as they considered him to be.

On the cold and bleak morning of November 9, when the march commenced, large numbers of onlookers and journalists were present to witness the events, just as Hitler had intended by his actions the previous night at the Bürgerbräukeller. As the group marched towards the war memorial—knowing full well that a conflict taking place there would be considered an act of heresy by the security forces—the police played right into into the hands of Hitler and the National Socialists as they began shooting at the marchers. The marchers in the front rank stood their ground in the direct line of fire, and this included Adolf Hitler, front and centre. This was to be his threshold moment no matter what occurred, and what happened next became a modern Nazi *Grail* epic in the years to come. When the person standing directly beside him was shot dead, Hitler was dragged down by the dying man as he fell. The majority of the witnesses, which included the police and all of Hitler's comrades, were unified in praising his bravery during the shootings. The mythology that Hitler 'belly flopped' like a coward and shielded himself behind his injured comrades can be only sourced through reports written by opposing Marxist journalists and propaganda outlets. Adolf Hitler may have been an appalling and monstrous individual, but the reality remains that on that morning in Munich his bravery was noted even by neutral observers.

Sixteen party members were killed by the security forces, with dozens more injured, including Hermann Goering who took a bullet in the groin and was ironically treated by a Jewish doctor after a

Gentile doctor refused him help. When Hitler was arrested two days later, he was already considered a hero by many of the citizens of Munich. He had attained the epic battle victory he needed, and along with this, through the sacrifice of his comrades, gave birth to the central magical rite of the National Socialists; the *'Ritual of the Blood Banner'*.

THE SECULAR WITCHCRAFT TRIAL

At the end of his trial in relation to charges made in the wake of the Munich Putsch of November 8-9, 1923, Adolf Hitler had become a living hero to millions of Germans for his bravery and conviction to his cause and his comrades. He was no longer merely a regional politician in the south of the country, but also a knight with a wizard-like ability to survive certain death as bullets crashed into others all around him as he marched defiantly onwards for Germany. This is precisely how the people of Bavaria viewed the situation, and the follow-up court case only entrenched his public image. Hardly surprising then that Adolf Hitler and other members of the National Socialists Party received the minimum sentence possible. However, this was to be no mere prison sentence.

Hitler's imprisonment was to be portrayed in epic terms by the emerging Nazi propaganda machine as a knight entering into exile in order to return with the Holy Grail. Hitler and his coven had performed a successful magical ritual that the entire world had taken notice of. The time had come to prepare for the second ritual: the creation of the supernatural empire of the Third Reich.

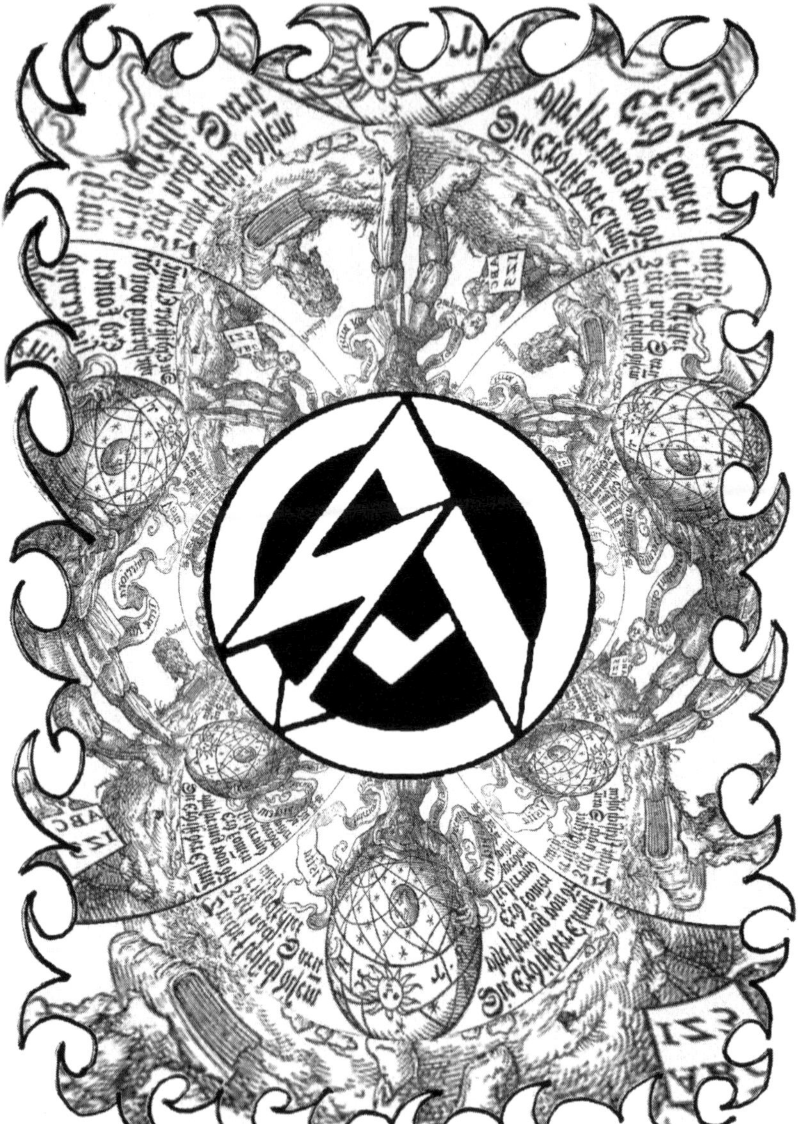

ELEVEN

INVOCATION

"Hitler's thoughts were as if they had been taken from the Law of Thelema."

— Aleister Crowley

To fully understand why Hitler and the Thulists manifested precisely the results they desired from the events in Munich during late 1923, we must first look to the crucial importance of the myths and epics infused within the Germanic consciousness, and how this mystical, nationalistic self-identity was almost akin to a narcotic fix craved by the German people in the years after the Great War. A desire for the romantic and magical quests for racial and cultural redemption, as real in terms of their day-to-day practical needs such as food, clothing and shelter. It is one thing for people to live a pragmatic existence concerned only with their daily survival. However, without a mystical framework on which to pin these cold realities, life has very little meaning beyond the need to remain in existence. Germans had been culturally indoctrinated to believe that heroes and knights embarking on epic quests and gallant adventures—even with expressions of cruel and vindictive slaughter against their foes—were as meaningful as the price of a loaf of bread in Bavaria or election ballot results in Saxony.

WAGNER AND THE GRAIL MYSTERIES

If Adolf Hitler's magical incantations and rituals created the Third Reich, then the instinctual magician Richard Wagner summoned up Adolf Hitler from his own will, using the art and science of opera. Wagner's operas were the psychedelic musical entheogen of Hitler's hatred of the Jews and his belief in the superiority of German blood. Hitler once stated that in the music of Wagner's *Rheingold*, the scientists of the future would discover the secrets of presently unknown forces of motion and force. This is an incredible statement. Here is Adolf Hitler declaring Wagner to be a kind of musical sorcerer in an age long before the full understanding of sound waves and how they affect the natural world were completely understood. The use of acoustics, musical notation sequences and changing pitches to alter the nature of consciousness and even matter, was, however, long understood within occult circles. Hitler knew how

Wagner's music affected him personally, and therefore he wanted to harness the emotional and psychological effects of Wagner's music for his own ends.

The music of Wagner provided a kind of visionary stage in the mind of Hitler, which eventually he would bring into material existence. There is no doubt that Wagner was a musical genius, and his uses of sweeping tones and his groundbreaking precise coordination with lighting and stage effects remains as spellbinding today as it did back then. The effects of Wagner's music upon Adolf Hitler's behaviour was observed first-hand by the visiting American journalist Frederick Oechsner, who stated that he witnessed 'grimaces of pain and pleasure contort his face, his brows knit, his eyes close, his mouth contracting tightly'.

From my research into psychopathology, I have discovered that psychopaths rarely, if ever, develop a true emotional relationship with the subtle nuances and beauty of music. This is one of the factors which makes Adolf Hitler a mystery and probably always will remain so. His pathology towards treating millions of humans as garbage to be disposed of is indeed psychopathic, along with his need to manipulate the perceptions of others for his own requirements is, likewise, stock and trade of the psychopath. At the same time, however, Adolf Hitler seemed to have a genuine sense of human 'completeness' at times which psychopaths *never* demonstrate, such as a genuine love and emotional resonance with art and beauty beyond that of trying to look or act cultured.

This presented me with a paradox concerning Hitler and his obsession with Wagner, until I came across this report from Frederick Oechsner. Oechsner was describing Adolf Hitler in a state of 'possession' and not as an expression of a real love of music. Wagner's music allowed Hitler to more effectively communicate with the demons—whatever these demons were precisely—within his being. Adolf Hitler also used the music of Wagner to invoke certain demonic archetypes—or walk-ins—in the same manner that the Siberian shaman uses the constant rhythm of a drum to allow himself to become a receptacle for another spirit. Again, this is speculative, and when I use terms such as 'demons' and 'possession', I am talking strictly in terms of pathological poles of the psyche unleashing certain negative archetypes.

If the reader wishes to replace this rationalisation with actual demon possession in order to understand the sheer inhumanity of Adolf Hitler, then I can hardly blame them. We are so far beyond the pale of understanding when trying to come to terms with comprehending Hitler and the Third Reich, even if we are applying the magical and occult framework to this horrific period of human history. Something transformed Hitler from a proto-psychopath to a full-blown psychopath, and only a total reorganisation of his being would have achieved this. Something very dark and powerful indeed, and Wagner's music was key to Hitler's supreme occult evil. While still a teenager in Linz, immediately after attending a performance of *Rienzi, the Last of the Tribunes*, Hitler and his friend August Kubizek together ascended up the slopes of the Freinberg, a mountain on the outskirts of the city and incredibly, Adolf Hitler—a provincial nobody at the time—presented his friend with his vision of a Third Reich which was to come to pass almost word for word, if Kubizek's story is to believed.

THE MUSICAL BLACK MASS

Beyond the actual music itself, Wagner's stage productions, costumes, use of lighting effects and themes entrenched the heroic archetypes into the consciousness of Hitler long after the performance ended. So much so, that Hitler and the Third Reich can be seen as a pathological on-going expression of Wagner after the curtain falls and the opera house empties. The Germanic mythology and desires for redemption encapsulated in the heroic struggles of *Riezi, Stolzing, Tannhauser* and most importantly of all, *Siegfried*, infused into the psychology of Hitler the potential of Germany's own living epic of sacrifice, betrayal and salvation, all taking place under

Hitler's spell. The common motif within the narrative of Wagner's operas is the obscure outsider who changes everything in the course of a heroic quest. Wagner and Hitler shared so many similarities in this regard. Both had no formal academic education in the chosen arts. Both were anti-Semites. Both were vegetarians.

It was almost as if some demonic force had created a school of sorcery on this planet and it reached its culmination when the demons behind the veil passed their baton from Wagner and on to Hitler in order to put their energy-harvesting plans into action. Such an idea is not that unusual, as both within the Gnostic tradition and the Cathars (both of which influenced the Germanic mystical orders) believed that non-human demonic beings created situations in the material world such as wars and religious conflicts, in order to feed energy back into the demon world. Hitler himself stated, while declaring Wagner to be the greatest prophet of the German people, "With the exception of Richard Wagner, I have no forerunner." Hitler was the sorcerer's apprentice. As he entered prison, what Hitler needed now was his own Wagnerian opera company to construct the greatest stage performance possible in the minds of the German people: The Third Reich.

THE HERO IN EXILE

Following the sensational trial of Adolf Hitler, where he proclaimed that among other things irrelevant to the actual events of the Munich Putsch of November 8-9, he cried with pride at the grave of Richard Wagner, while also proclaiming that the mothers of Germany would entrust National Socialism to safeguard their sons, Hitler was found guilty and then left the courtroom to the cries of "Heil Hitler!" This was the first time a large group had chanted this mantra while in a hypnotic state of hysteria, which they carried into the streets of Munich later that evening. Adolf Hitler announced to them that the "Goddess of the Eternal Court of History" would absolve him of the guilty verdict as he was taken away to spend nine months in prison gestating his cult of personality behind bars, in order to be reborn as a national hero and saviour of his people.

MEIN KAMPF – THE BOOK OF NAZI LAW

In 1924, while in prison following a lenient sentence handed down by a sympathetic right-wing court in Munich, Adolf Hitler set about writing his visionary book of ritual magic that was needed to bring his pathological will into fruition. The culmination of the half-dozen years since his hospital bed magical experience provided him with his 'mission' to save Germany. This was to be his book of spells and enchantment; *Mein Kampf* (*My Struggle*). A book which is nothing less than a prophetic saga with Adolf Hitler in the guise of a 20th century Teutonic knight, complete with magical abilities, slaying the dragons with his *Weltanschauung*, or his all-encompassing philosophical world view. The book was later to become the Black-Häxan-Paganism bible of the Reich. At the time, however, very few people viewed *Mein Kampf* in such terms, with the imporant exception of Adolf Hitler's fellow prison inmate Rudolf Hess, who was present during every word Hitler issued.

Hess was rarely away from Hitler's side while they both served their prison sentences together in a prison that was more akin to a resort, as gifts and well wishes from admirers all over the world arrived on a daily basis. Hess frantically typed *Mein Kampf* as Hitler dictated the book to him, standing and walking around the cell in a state of near messianic zeal. The closeness of the relationship between Hitler and Hess was seen by some as being latently homosexual. Hess, being in Hitler's cell until late at night, only compounded these rumours. However, these accusations appear groundless and are perhaps based on jealousy inflicted upon Hess by other members of the inner Nazi circle who resented the closeness of the bond between Hess and Hitler. Their relationship over the coming years was to take on epic proportions, and one which is still deeply mysterious in nature.

While not a homosexual relationship between Hitler and Hess—repressed or otherwise—a hint of their connection being more akin to Hess' occult influence on his fellow inmate was cryptically revealed one night in prison during a full moon when the future Führer, looking up at the lunar sphere said to his future Deputy Führer, "...it's only the moon I hate. For it is something dead, and terrible, and inhuman. And human beings are afraid of it...it is as in the moon a part of terror still lives which the moon once sent down to earth...I hate it! That pale and ghastly fellow." What Hitler meant about something inside or about the moon which affects human affairs is difficult to speculate upon. On some level, Hitler is implying that messages are being sent to earth from the moon itself, as the mentally ill often claim is the case. In this case, Hitler's hatred of the moon is intriguing, considering how he compared himself at times to a wolf. The moon—generally considered to represent that of the feminine aspect of the psyche—is also noticeable by its absence from both Nazi and Thulist symbolism.

Mein Kampf presents Hitler caught in a state of bombastic rapture as that of a great statesman in bloom who has freed himself from the shackles of intellectualism while offering a polemic that would not only stir the ordinary German out of their slumber, but call them to join Hitler, the Teutonic knight, on his mystical quest. Within a decade, *Mein Kampf* was to officially replace the *Holy Bible* as the religious book of the German race, and it would be quoted as scripture by millions. The book was written due to Hitler and the other Nazi inmates enjoying concessions as a political prisoner at Landsberg am Lech.

Hitler dictated *Mein Kampf* to Rudolf Hess as a stream of consciousness, who then committed it to paper using a Remington typewriter, as a gramophone played Wagner constantly in the background. The original title of the book was to be *Four and One Half Years of Battle Against Lies, Stupidity and Cowardice: Account Settled*. This overblown and simplistic title was changed to *Mein Kampf* at the suggestion of the Nazi politician and journalist Max Amann, and the first volume was completed by the time Hitler left prison. The strange, almost mantra-like punctuated style of the syntax contained within *Mein Kampf* has been incorrectly judged as poorly written by literary critics ever since its publication.

They have completely missed the point. *Mein Kampf* is a book of enchantment designed to hammer home the message into the consciousness of the reader. Consider the following passage, and if possible, read it aloud in the style of an incantation or prayer in order to understand what Hitler was conveying to the reader:

'The concept of völkisch in consequence of its boundlessness, is not a possible foundation for movement and offers no measure for the membership of such a movement. The more practically undefinable this conception is, the more and freer interpretation it permits, the more increases also the possibility of having recourse to it. The insertion into the political fight of so undefinable a conception, interpretable in so many senses, leads to the diminution, interpretable in so many senses, leads to the dimutation of every energetic fighting unity, as it is incompatible with this to leave to the individual the definition of his faith and his will. For this reason it is a disgrace to see in these days who drift about with the word völkisch on their caps.'

Clearly this is classic psychopathic word salad, as Hitler offers us his bewildering views on the *völkisch* Germanic romantic folklore and racial movement from which the Nazis derived their own momentum. It is word salad, but word salad with a purpose, along with some suspiciously occult-sounding phrases, perhaps due to Rudolf 'dear Rudi' Hess, or the Jesuit Father Bernard Stempfle, who edited the first edition of *Mein Kampf* (for reasons not fully understood), and who was later murdered under Hitler's orders. In *Mein Kampf*, as is the case with many cult leaders, Hitler is killing the modern layer of the Germanic psyche and unleashing the dark forces below. However, it is done in such a manner that the reader is both spellbound but also bewildered. The idea is to take the reader so far by generating a sense of anticipation, and then not delivering the answer they were hoping for. This is to keep the reader hooked and coming back for more answers. The cult leader aspect of this approach is clearly seen in this line:

"Whoever has not himself been on the tentacles of this throttling viper will never know its fangs."

Vipers have neither tentacles nor do they asphyxiate their prey. The imagery is not ignorance; it is conjunctive metaphor linking imagery within the mind of the reader targeting the reptilian lower brain of the reader in order to place them in a state of hyper-vigilance. This would be then turned into a battle cry, and would in time be described by *Gestapo* founder Hermann Göring as being "written on the faces of the marching stormtroopers." While the *völkisch* of the 19th century conceptualised the German psyche within an almost agrarian and rustic framework, *Mein Kampf* set about to industrialise Germanic racial identity within a Black-Häxan-Paganism framework, and it did so by using overtly occult language and techniques. It could not have been done by any other means.

THE GRIMOIRE OF CHAOS

It was James Joyce who set about "to forge the uncreated conscience" of the Irish race, and in some perverse way, Adolf Hitler set about the same idea with the Germanic uncreated consciousness. Rather than free them from religious guilt and oppression as Joyce intended with the Irish, Hitler was determined to unleash the demons of the tortured Germanic psyche and give birth to a kind of *Frankenstein* monster within the collective German consciousness which he could use to forge his own vision. However, while James Joyce was a brilliant author, Adolf Hitler had a very different agenda with *Mein Kampf*; his was a rant with a purpose, and very similar in delivery to that of British occultist Aleister Crowley, the *Great Beast 666* himself.

Hardly surprising then, when Crowley later proclaimed his 'Do What Thou Wilt' philosophy had been adopted by Hitler while claiming that he quoted from Crowley's *The Book of the Law,* concerning a new age of magic being brought into fruition through will. According to John Symmonds in *The Medusa's Head*, Hitler had personally contacted Crowley, asking him if he was an angel of darkness, to which the Great Beast is alleged to have replied. "If I were an angel of light, you wouldn't want to know me." If this dialogue actually took place as Symmonds claims, then here is the *Great Beast* himself declaring that Hitler was involved in black magic.

What a vast and complex vision Hitler provides within the pages of *Mein Kampf*, and a terrifyingly consistent one at that. The book represents nothing less than a declaration of war upon the psyche of the reader, and then demands of the reader to choose his side of the battlefield, or else be prepared to be mutilated upon the breaking wheel of National Socialism. The Black-Häxan-Pagan mindset of Hitler literally screams off every page, as his unforgiving and nihilistic world view presents an almost Gothic landscape of Darwinian harshness coupled with the brutality of the Middle Ages. The underlying message being consistently conveyed was that: *the strong must survive and the weak must perish*. A completely black and white world view with no liberal grey areas for the 'weak' to find refuge within. Consider the following statement from Hitler and remind yourself that you are reading something that was written in the 20th century and not the Middle Ages:

"Those who want to live let them fight, and those who do not want to fight in this world of eternal struggle do not deserve to live."

Like all good magicians, Hitler was informing the target of his intentions, so no one could accuse him of not being direct and upfront with them. Hitler knew that Germany lacked a meaningful religion, that even the *völkisch* was essentially secular, and that its rituals were hardly going to resurrect the sleeping Teutonic dragons in significant numbers. Christianity had long been central to German life until the *Enlightenment*, and there were the after-effects of an enormous spiritual vacuum among the population in this regard. In the pages of *Mein Kampf*, Adolf Hitler delivers to them the new state religion of National Socialism coupled with the concept that German Aryan blood is sacred and does not need the *Transubstantiation* of the Catholic Mass in order to make it magical.

Hitler makes it clear that Germanic blood was once magical, and then had been corrupted by racial mixing and loss of national identity. Hitler does not promise life after death, but he could promise the reader the status of a living god to any German willing to follow his mission. The message was that this is the only life we have, the only life we will ever know, and the Germanic bloodline must struggle to fight or perish. To Hitler, life was nothing more than the powerful destroying the meek, and that this was the natural order of things, so why deny it? This is the very core belief of European Black-Häxan-Paganism and it is all over the pages of *Mein Kampf*.

CULTURAL SURVIVAL AS THE ONLY TRUTH

German philosophy in the decades since the death of Nietzsche had become consumed with the school of *Phenomenology*, which stated that study of experience and consciousness was an almost mechanical idea, in that reality is viewed as objects, and these objects acting and reacting upon one another are perceived in consciousness. The German philosopher Martin Heidegger speculated that only by acts of free choice divorced from anxiety can people have some promise of authenticity. Heidegger's belief was that we are thrown into this life, and then we are determined by the roles others inflict upon us. This view allowed Nazi-inclined intellectuals to validate their choice of supporting National Socialism, in that Heidegger maintained that only by committing oneself to their own national identity and culture and abiding by it completely could life have any real purpose. This validation of cultural and nationalist 'mob rule' creates authentic personalities who know precisely what was required from them in this life. Such a philosophy would have been embraced eagerly by the Nazis, as well as used by intellectuals, as a rationale to support the *Hitler Party*.

Hitler also wrote *Mein Kampf* at a time when Darwinian ideas had essentially triumphed and began to enter into social policy in most 'advanced' nations during this period. In the United States, the implementation of forced selective sterilisation of African-Americans and poor whites was becoming the main scientific and social policy of the day. Hitler's ideas surrounding the sanctity of blood and race would not have been considered radical nor immoral at all to most educated people at the time. In fact, the majority of university professors and intellectuals would have embraced them as common sense and important social policy. This universal scientific acceptance of Eugenics gave Adolf Hitler a 'rational' mandate for the Aryan race to strive towards becoming the most superior and noble on the planet.

At a time when Germans were looking for hope, dignity and salvation from the humiliation of the Versailles Treaty, this idea would have been seductive, if not intoxicating to millions standing in line for bread or selling their bodies for medicine. Coupling this personal and social humiliation with Heidegger's 'authentic' life, led invariably to the destruction of the individual for the good of the Germanic racial community, and this was to become considered as being the most noble manner in which to live one's life. Not as a sovereign and independent being, but as a single repository of Germanic blood which was carried and cherished by the individual who contained this powerful life force within their own blood. This supernatural repository of Aryan blood was, when isolated individually, no more important than the collective racial pool of the Germanic master race. This blood, which must be passed on as a racially pure elixir to the next generation as soon as possible, through selective reproduction and kept pure with successive generations.

Kept pure until a Vril-ya type race of super-beings emerges among the German and Aryan races.

Consequently, if one is to be called upon to sacrifice oneself in battle to defend the Fatherland, they are but one drop in an ocean that will continue to live on forever with each successive generation of Germans evolving towards eventual racial perfection. Thus, the creation of pure Aryan children, according to *Mein Kampf,* takes on a spiritual dimension. Hitler's words were offering readers practical steps on how to live forever; the results of which were scientifically veritable and not just articles of faith. Every mind-control and flying saucer religious cult has used a similar template of behavioural control, sacrifice of individual will, along with the means to transcend death, and that is what Adolf Hitler offered in *Mein Kampf.*

FEARS OF A RESURRECTED GOLEM

As with all good heroic sagas, an oppressive enemy is required to be defeated, and for Hitler, this was the Jews. *Mein Kampf* is a declaration of war upon Jewry, which pulls no punches in terms of dealing with their presence in Europe. Although Hitler was careful to tone down some of his more inflammatory statements which he issued back in Munich in 1919 when he referred to the Jews as a "racial tuberculosis", the now philosophical statesman Adolf Hitler resorted to less colourful and degrading terms such as 'parasites' and 'spongers'. By coupling Judaism with Communism in the same manner as the Thule Society had done in 1919, this provided Hitler with a 'legitimate' mandate to invade the lands to the East and return them back to the German people. Deviously psychopathic in terms of how Hitler copperfastens racial hatreds with strategic and political objectives by placing the racial enemy within the boundaries of the lands which are to be conquered or liberated, as Hitler and his supporters made it seem.

The primary and deadly Black-Häxan-Paganism spell of *Mein Kampf*, and what made it so influential if not hypnotic to the reader, was that what appears on the surface to be bombastic and even corny concepts of race, sacrifice and conquest when read in English (or any other language) comes across very differently when Hitler's manifesto is read in German. Very few outside Germany took *Mein Kampf* seriously before 1938-39. The Italian dictator Mussolini stated it was so boring that he could not finish reading it. The non-German versions of *Mein Kampf* read as the obsessive histrionics of an unstable mind, rather than the work of a great statesman.

Everything within *Mein Kampf* is connected to blood in one way or another. Politics, foreign diplomacy, economics, education and even the arts, all fall within a framework of horrific ambition that seems deluded to outsiders, and, more importantly, mythological in both scale and emotional quality to Hitler's followers. *Mein Kampf,* under Hitler's orders, was never translated into English by his publishers, and most of the English versions floating around were highly edited for propaganda purposes to make them seem especially absurd and as overblown as possible.

THE SHOCK DOCTRINE

Years later, in 1939, when it seemed as if war with Germany was an absolute certainty, British officials and intelligence services finally began to read the original German version of *Mein Kampf*—by assuming within themselves a Germanic consciousness of understanding—in order to get inside Hitler's head, and in particular, the heads of his millions of devoted followers. What they discovered shocked and frightened many of them. On the surface, what reads as a trashy, if not crazed polemic in English, expresses itself as a magical saga when read in German, and seemed completely convincing.

More importantly, they began to understand that *Mein Kampf* was written and phrased in more of an archaic form of the German language or '*Low German*' (*Plattdeutsch*), with its very ancient origins in *Old Saxon* dialect, the language of the Teutonic witches.

The same ancient tongue of the primordial Teutonic woodlands proportedly uttered by the spirits of Prince von Thurn und Taxis and Countess von Westarp at the Thule Society seance back in 1919.

Following the *First Orthographical Conference* in 1876 (*I. Orthographische Konferenz*) implemented by the Prussian government to standardise German spelling across all of Germany, Austria and other Germanic communities around central Europe, the distinction between spoken and written German became seamless. German officialdom wrote what it said, and said what it wrote. However, on a more archetypal level, many ordinary Germans were still cognitively processing their emotions and inclinations using '*Low German*', the language of the deep and dark Germanic psyche. When Hitler and Rudolf Hess wrote *Mein Kampf* (edited by a Jesuit priest no less) in cell number 7 at Landsberg, they were using the syntax and narrative of a pre-*Enlightenment* version of German.

Then, as now, academics and intellectuals claim that *Mein Kampf* is merely a badly written diatribe authored by nothing more than a raving, bombastic lunatic. In reality, *Mein Kampf* is a book purposely written to cause academics to dismiss it, and by doing so, remain ignorant of the spells contained within the syntax, as Hitler (or more likely Hess) created *Mein Kampf* to shoot straight to the reptilian complex in order to release the ghosts of the Teutonic groves and forests. *Mein Kampf* is very much a book of magical spells designed to cause change within the modern German psyche of the masses, by returning them—in an archetypal sense—to a time of nocturnal fears and endless winters filled with danger and predators hidden in the shadows, and then, from this, offering them the potential for the first dawn of a Germanic springtime. *Mein Kampf* was their beacon of hope and restoration.

In the years to come, it would seem as if Hitler possessed an almost Nostradamus-like level of ability to 'predict' the future and then make it happen before the eyes of his people in real time. As impressive and startling as this was to the British intelligence services reading *Mein Kampf* (which by that time, it was too late), one can only imagine the effect the book would have had on the consciousness of a young German who may have read the book soon after Hitler left prison in 1924. He or she would have believed they were living within an unfolding magical Wagnerian saga which came to pass as the prophet Adolf Hitler had predicted it would. Then, following this realisation of Hitler as the living German redeemer, the readers of *Mein Kampf* would do anything he required from them, as they knew the Führer had always been correct about everything else.

Hitler had successfully changed the consciousness of the readers of *Mein Kampf* into conformity with his own will. The book of rituals and spells which was *Mein Kampf* came to pass before the eyes of the reader, and the proof was undeniable. The Germans finally had their own bible. All they needed to do now was to avoid the inevitable asphyxiation by the vipers during the remaining Germanic winter nights, which only Hitler could lead them out of.

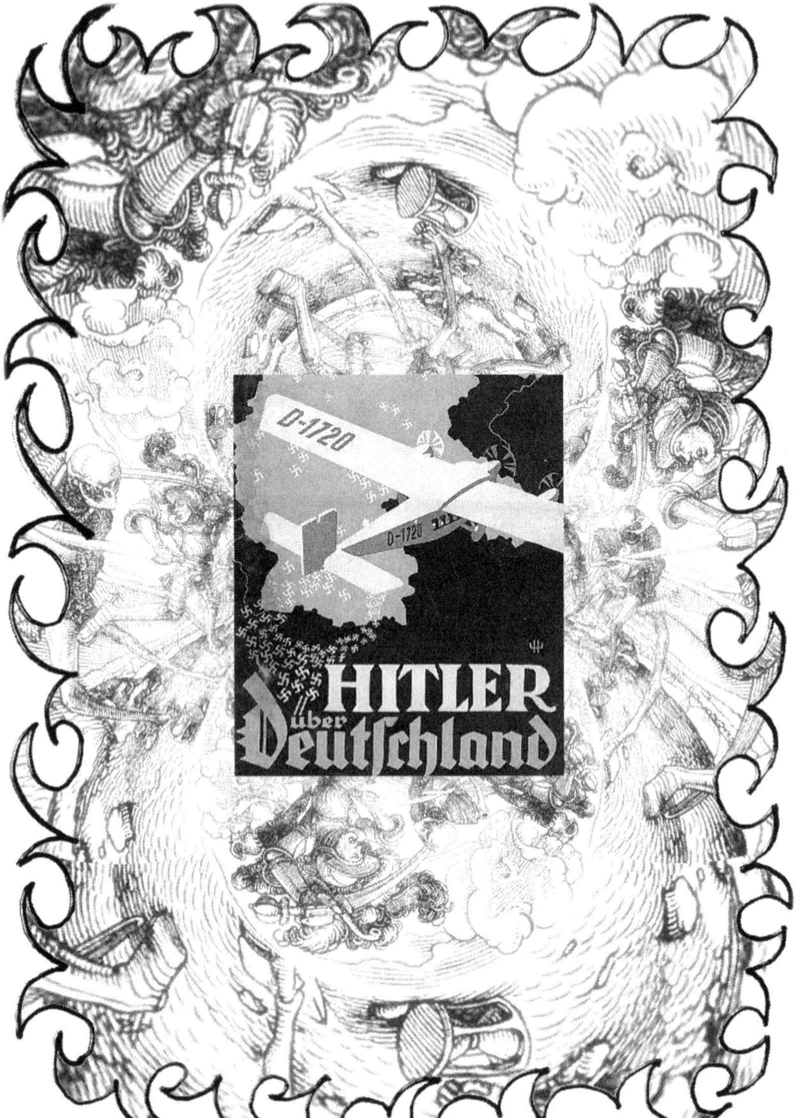
D-1720
HITLER
über
Deutschland

TWELVE

LEVITATION

"The historian is a prophet facing backwards."

— Friedrich von Schlegel

The last great recognised painting of the *Symbolist* arts movement is generally considered to be *Judith*, by Hitler's favourite artist, Franz von Stuck. Completed in 1924, and just in time for Hitler's release from Landsberg prison, it is based on the story from the *Old Testament* in the *Book of Judith*, which in the German Lutheran tradition forms part of the *Apocrypha*, implying Jewish religious stories which are of dubious authenticity, or with hidden or suspect motives. The *Book of Judith* tells the story of Holofernes, the military commander of the Assyrian king Nebuchadnezzar, who was seduced and then decapitated by the beautiful widow named Judith while his army lay siege to Jerusalem.

What makes this painting so interesting is that it serves as a cultural insight of sorts into the fears and collective neurosis of the Germans at the time. The imagery in the painting is that of the naked Jewess, Judith, taking one last satisfied glance of the sleeping Holofernes, while holding the sword she is about to behead him with. In the representation of *Judith* by von Stuck, she is sporting a 1920s style haircut, which was typical of women of the Berlin artistic/bohemian scene of the era. Judith, holding her sword ready to slaughter a sleeping man, represented all that the growing nationalist movement of 1920s Germany both loathed and feared. Millions of neurotic and emotionally vulnerable Germans at that time would have identified with Holofernes, and the National Socialists played on the paranoia surrounding their own Apocrypha of the Jews and intellectuals in post-Great War Germany. Many felt that the Germans were asleep, awaiting the same fate as Holofernes; 'The epitome of depraved seduction...' as one German journalist later described the painting.

Following the publication of *Mein Kampf* and Hitler's release from prison, the Nazi party was in a state of decline. In order to reverse this situation, Hitler decided that working within the context of the *Weimar Constitution*, the party could attain power through the electoral ballot rather than the bullet. Once in power, they would take steps to outlaw all other parties and politicians, and thereby ending democracy in Germany for the next one thousand years. With *Mein*

Kampf in one hand, and while vowing to crush the enemies of Germany with a clenched fist in the other, the transformation of an occult-paramilitary operation into a legitimate (on the surface) democratic political party, infused with overt concepts of racial faith and destiny, the solution would be: 'Hitler is Germany, and Germany is Hitler'. The back-stabbing Judith would eventually have to be removed from Germany, so Holofernes could safely awaken from his slumber.

It was around this time that the more occult science aspects came to the public fore within the culture of National Socialism. Hitler constantly told his followers to put their faith ahead of their intellect. However, practical matters concerning the financial health of the *Hitler Party* still needed to be dealt with, so Hitler consulted his 'dear Rudi' once again to solve the financial issues surrounding the now democratic National Socialist movement. The period between 1924 and 1933 witnessed the rise of Adolf Hitler as a major world figure, while Rudolf Hess took care of the 'backstage' esoteric realities of National Socialism, which included placing Joseph Goebbels—a complex and interesting figure—as the Nazi regional party leader in Berlin, where his brilliant and intensive propaganda skills were used to undermine not only the aloof intelligentsia of Berlin society, but also to destroy morale among members of the Social Democratic and Communist parties in the city government. Attending to the practical matters of enticing urban working class people into the National Socialist Party, Goebbels created an image of practicality and national security at the core of the party to distract the populace from the continuation, if not (hidden) deeper entrenchment of the Black-Häxan-Paganism within the party structure and culture.

THE ALCHEMICAL ENGAGEMENT

In July 1919, inspired by the developments taking place at the Four Seasons Hotel in Munich, members of a Theosophically-inclined occult French group called *Affranchis*, renamed and reorganised themselves as *Les Veilleurs* ("the Vigilants") set themselves up as a similar occult-political movement similar to the Thulists in Bavaria. Among their members was none other than Rudolf Hess, who can be clearly seen in a group photo taken of the group. This mystical-political collective published its manifesto in December 1919, advising all Jews living in France to "go back home".

Les Veilleurs appeared to have had a knowledge of alchemy which the Germanic Thulists (and other German occultists) also appeared to have had a strong interest in, and so Hess called upon the assistance of occult poet and *Les Veilleurs* comrade R. A. Schwaller de Lubicz, or 'Aor' as he referred to himself, who was in possession of a valuable alchemical manuscript of great importance. The experiments resulted in gold being processed from lead using a 'red powder' according to the instructions given in the manuscript at a small laboratory inside a gasworks during 1914. Hess' involvement with *Les Veilleurs* inspired the Nazis to take alchemy seriously again as a means of raising funds for the party.

As Hitler and Hess were preparing themselves to leave prison and take command of the National Socialists once again, Franz Tausen, a chemist in Munich, produced a document entitled *180 Elements, the Atomic Weight, and Their Incorporation in the System of Harmonic Periods*. According to Tausen, every element contains its own unique vibration of energy and frequency directly related to the atomic weight of the nucleus and its orbiting electrons. Tausen then proposed that all matter in the universe could be 'orchestrated' by modifying its orbital elements which would transmute one form of matter into the other. Within Munich esoteric circles, excited rumours circulated that Tausen had successfully created gold from base metal using his techniques. He was then approached by the Nazi treasurer, General Erich von Ludendorff, and a demonstration was performed for the General, along with a delegation from the party, including a chemical engineer, to validate the authenticity of the experiments. Using iron oxide and quartz melted into a crucible, it was then kept in a hotel room with Tausen overnight. The next morning, using an electric furnace, the crucible was reheated, and more powder was added and left to cool. The results amazed the delegation, as a sizeable gold nugget fell out of the vessel.

Almost immediately, General von Lunderdorff created Company 164 with the expressed brief to produce gold for the Nazi Party. Officially, no reports of gold being created at the factory were issued until 1928, but this is not to say that the process had failed up until that point. It would not have been wise for Hitler and the Nazis to reveal that his own and the party's sudden and very obvious increase in personal wealth was a result of successful alchemical processes. The Nazis, as with any cult, had a tendency to use the services of individuals and then dispose of them when they were no longer required in such a manner as to destroy the credibility of their former servants. Tausen was eventually very publicly destroyed during a high profile trial in 1931, even after it was proved that in a single experiment he had indeed produced 723 grams of pure gold. The Nazis had their finances sorted by then, and Franz Tausen—a classic example of an educated useful idiot procured by the Nazi cult—was now deemed surplus to their requirements, and was left to the mercy of the courts.

THE SEDUCTION GAME

In 1920, the French military began placing sub-Saharan African troops in control of the occupied Rhineland as an antagonistic measure to police the German population, and soon afterwards reports came in that these troops were raping German women on a routine basis. In some cases, this appears to have happened, while in other instances, racial fears of half-caste pregnancies—known at the time as the 'Black Shame'—resulted in some German women who were in romantic relationships with black French troops, claiming rape to avoid the social embarrassment. Even so, German Catholic leaders wrote to the French military, requesting that these African troops be removed from the Rhineland and replaced with white French and Belgian soldiers.

France's ambassador to the Holy See dismissed these stories as "odious propaganda", and the French military further cultivated racial hysteria among Rhineland German civilians by proclaiming that more black troops were being sent to the region. Eventually, the Holy See took the matter up with the British, who managed to influence the French military enough for them to remove the African Allied troops in order to reduce tension in the Rhineland. The damage had already been done, and Germany was even more neurotic about 'contamination' of Teutonic blood from Africans. This played perfectly into the hands of the National Socialists.

THE ECUMENICAL ANTICHRIST

Adolf Hitler, now free from prison and restructuring the Nazis as a democratic party, was acutely aware of the influence of the Catholic Church as a powerful resistance force within Germany to National Socialism. The German bishops' ability to have black French troops removed from the Rhineland through their powerful and influential diplomatic channels did not go unnoticed. Hitler and the Nazis were to be the only 'spiritual' identity for their vision of a Third Reich, and a confrontation with the German Catholic church was inevitable. In an editorial Hitler wrote for the February 26, 1925 edition of the newspaper *Völkischer Beobachter*, he stated that National Socialism would not be dragged into religious disputes, and that the Catholic church in Germany had nothing to fear from either him or his party.

A few weeks later, at a public meeting, Hitler—not unexpectedly—vowed to eradicate all forms of Christianity from German life, issuing the ultimatum that one is "either a Christian or a German. You can't be both." At the same time, Hitler was using Nazi sympathisers within the German Catholic church as spies, through which he became aware of the full extent of the "immense technical apparatus" of the Holy See. Hitler was also aware that the Catholic and other Christian churches in Germany were losing millions of their flock, and by his understanding and employing the methodologies of the technical apparatus of the Holy See, he would be able to lure these lapsed Catholics and Protestants into the new state religion of National Socialism, once the required 'spiritual' structures were in place to do so.

This was precisely what Hitler had outlined in *Mein Kampf* when he had mocked the *völkisch* movement. He needed the Germanic racial and cultural movements to become the grassroots of a new religion —based on a cult of blood, force and will—for a resurgent Germany in order to remove Christianity from German life, while infusing Black-Häxan-Paganism into every aspect of German society; from the day-to-day bureaucracy to the military and into the homes and lifestyles of the civilian population. This would include replacing Christian holidays and festivals with National Socialist holidays and celebrations, which were to be generally in and around occultic nature-worshipping periods of Teutonic antiquity.

HIGH SOCIETY

Hitler was now living in a luxurious new apartment in the fashionable Bogenhausen neighbourhood of Munich, enjoying lavish banquets where Wagner's music boomed out constantly to entertain his growing coterie of admirers, including film stars along with powerful business and media connections. At these banquets were

Nazis of the high-ranking inner circle, who had their own 'theme' music played as they entered the rooms. Hitler took this idea directly from Wagner's operas, where heroes and villains had suitable music scores in order to win either the hearts or hate of the audience. These events were glamourous, high society affairs, and the Nazis were indulged and toasted by the elite not just from Germany, but from elites all over the world who attended them, with guests ranging from United States senators, to British aristocracy. Despite the slick and well-oiled Nazi machine at the top, the grassroots of National Socialism was in a fractured and disorganised condition by the mid 1920s. While Hitler wined and dined with powerful friends, and slept with the many women and movie starlets who were flocking to his apartment, Captain Ernst Röhm was busily organising the grassroots of the party through his network and influence among military veterans, who were former *Freikorps,* while Dietrich Eckhart used his *Völkischer Beobachter* newspaper to push Adolf Hitler and National Socialism at every opportunity, constantly offering them up as the only antidote to the 'Jewish Problem'.

The National Socialists themselves, even as late as the mid 1920s, were still essentially a loose network of fractured alliances who only agreed upon one thing above all else: that Adolf Hitler was the only concrete element within the movement to unify them as a single political force on the national stage. Yet doubts persisted about who

Adolf Hitler really was and what he actually represented, even among some party members within the exclusive inner circle. There was always the question of his sudden wealth and affluent lifestyle. This was a concern to rank and file party members, while the inner core seemed unconcerned, as if they were aware of how Hitler had obtained this wealth as the 1920s progressed.

There are, and always have been, wealthy benefactors and overseas political supporters who provide all cults and potentially 'useful' political organisations with help in underwriting their financial needs. However, not to the extent where the Nazi party finances, along with Hitler's wealth, was so impressive and stable. Money was not a worry for National Socialists. Because of this, questions were being asked. Were there secret links to foreign businesses and banks supplying Hitler with funds as his star began to rise on the international stage? Perhaps it is also likely that Franz Tausen's *System of Harmonic Periods* had been yielding vast quantities of alchemical gold after all, and a cover story of disappointing results was leaked out to hide the real facts.

THE LAST STATION OF THE BROKEN CROSS

The journalists of the *Munich Post* newspaper, which was located at 19 Altheimer Eck, were the first group to discover that Adolf Hitler was a far more complex, colourful and interesting figure than his official humble origins suggested. Even if their often tabloid style diatribes towards the future leader of Germany were highly polemic from the early 1920s onwards, the *Munich Post* nonetheless carried non-stop attacks on Adolf Hitler, which were deeply troubling to both him and his emerging death cult. Constantly mocking Hitler, along with exposing the criminal and perverted nature of his followers, the *Munich Post* initially began their attacks on Hitler based solely on political motives, as the paper itself was essentially the propaganda wing of the Bavarian Socialist Party. The *Munich Post* so successfully managed to get under Hitler's skin to the point where he referred to the paper as the 'Poison Kitchen'.

More tellingly, the *Munich Post* knew something very dark and sinister about Hitler that would have ended his future prospects before the 1920s had barely begun. As is typical with cults, Hitler and his well-financed cronies continually tied the *Munich Post* up in court with constant charges of blackmail, fraud, con artistry, libel and endless lawsuits. The highly litigious and hysterical reaction by Hitler speaks volumes to this. The paper had something on Hitler far beyond a run of the mill sex scandal, or other kinds of editorial titillation. This game of tit-for-tat went on for over a decade, and provides some of the most conclusive proof that Hitler was the leader of a typical religious death cult, while providing the template for how all such similar cults operate right up until the present day: attack those who know the hidden past and dark secrets, before they get to tell the full story.

Cults always use constant slander in their own media, while their fanatical crazed thugs and mind-controlled minions run terror campaigns of intimidation, threats, gang stalking and vicious smear campaigns. The cult has to attack and keep on attacking any present or potential 'enemies' who might undermine the infallibility of the leadership. This also sends out a clear message to anyone inside the cult—who may be thinking of leaving and blowing the whistle—that they will get the same treatment or much worse. The *Munich Post*, and how Adolf Hitler waged war upon the paper tells us much. He was hiding something very damaging to his image.

This warning is also sent out (indirectly) to rank and file cult members: that they had better keep their own mouths closed tight if they knew what was good for them. A very typical example of how Hitler's cult followers received and then acted upon such messages disseminated within the organisation was the tragic story of a young idealistic teenage *SA* recruit named Herbert Hentsch, who was forced to repeatedly shout "Heil Hitler" as Brownshirts kicked him to death. When his mother's grief, and details of Herbert Hentsch's ritual sacrifice to Hitler were reported in the press, both she and her late son were subjected to a ruthless smear campaign from inside Hitler's propaganda circles. Again, this is typical of cult behaviour. Invoking libel laws are also constantly used by cults to hold back the real story long enough until the cult has enough power to annihilate the accusers and wipe them and their insights off the face of the earth for good. It rarely happens that any cult achieves this level of power, but Hitler succeeded during his rise to power due to the fact that he had much more than serious politics and money behind him. He was a pathological spiritual force of demonic proportion, and this was collectively infused by vicious osmosis into the Nazi party and its various wings. Although legally it was impossible for the *Munich Post* at the time to come out with the full story regarding Hitler's 'strangeness', speculation was still rife among the coffee houses of the city. This ranged from Hitler being a Jew to him being a homosexual, and, more tellingly, how he had easy access to such immediate political and financial clout whenever he needed it. Back then, as it still remains today, an understandable speculation of conspiracy exists surrounding cults and their hidden political and corporate benefactors. This narrative of conspiracy and speculation lies in how the *Munich Post* obtained Hitler's damning secrets about just how dark and shady Hitler's past actually was. It was continually leaked to them from inside his own circle.

In 1921, a document was sent to the editorial office entitled *Adolf*

Hitler, Traitor which stated that Hitler had an unearthly 'strangeness' about him when one encountered him personally and up close. Further, that he seemed rather 'alien' to the German people he claimed to speak on behalf of. Even more importantly, questions arose surrounding his seemingly inexhaustible financial clout at a time when Hitler had neither a job and Germany had barely an economy, apart from wealthy speculators dealing in scrap metals. The *Munich Post* could easily obtain details of Hitler's life of luxury and first class living with receipts from top hotels and restaurants procured from inside his own party via disgruntled members who noted that Hitler seemed a little too familiar with the good life to be just a humble working class painter.

All this must be seen in the context of that time, as poverty and unemployment increased in Germany. Anyone with wealth was not only envied, but was also seen as being secretive. Jews had secrets...their mysterious Kabbalah...Gypsies had secrets...all their gold jewellery and strange customs... Germans only had politicians and poverty. But some Germans also had secrets; the rich and the decadent. Most of the elite German business class were getting rich from stockpiling and then exporting copper and tin.

This would have been considered almost alchemical—turning base metal into foreign currency 'gold'—in a country where the unemployed would run out into the streets with knives and begin frantically hacking the warm flesh off any horse who had just dropped dead in order to obtain some form of protein. During the paramilitary events surrounding the short-lived Bavarian Soviet Republic, groups of citizens would follow mounted troops going into a fight so they could literally eat the horses after the animals were shot dead. In the mid 1920s, some Germans were still living like this, with no hope in sight. Eventually, due to Hitler's 'salvation', they would be eating the flower of Germany—their own children—in 1946 and 1947 during the eventual 'abyss' the spiritual forms of Prince von Thurn und Taxis and Countess von Westarp had warned the Thule Society about during that seance back in 1919.

Yet, among all this poverty and widespread economic destitution of the post-Great War era, Hitler appeared to be just like the merchants he constantly rallied against. The *Munich Post* were never at a loss to point this fact out. This troubled Hitler very deeply; so much so, that back during the height of the November 1923 putsch, Hitler removed his personal bodyguards—the *Strosstrupp* Hitler (later to become the *SS*)—and ordered them to ransack the offices of the newspaper. This was essentially his first *Kristallnacht.* Then, with typical psychopathic double standards, he claimed to be shocked by this attack on free speech. It was to be but the first assault on the paper by the National Socialists. Often, psychopathic cult leaders are unaware of their own double standards until a third party points this out. How often have we read about the cult leader who lives within a palatial mansion, French country chateau or multi-million dollar Malibu beach house, all the while preaching the virtues of hard work and frugal existence to their followers. Hitler was enjoying the same lifestyle as far back as the early 1920s, and some of his lesser brainwashed followers were unhappy about it.

In 1932, the *Munich Post* blew the lid open on Hitler's personal death squad, which was known within the Brownshirts as *Cell G*. The story went on to become an international sensation at the time, with details of ritualistic-style murders and reprisal killings while quoting Hitler's mantra that "nothing happens within the movement without my knowledge, approval and will". The paper carried the earliest insights into the dark sex magic rituals of the Nazis, which were later to become the spiritual canon of the emerging *SS* death cult in an article entitled *Sexual Life in the Third Reich;* a report painting a very different picture from the wholesome family image which Hitler's cult was eager to disseminate to the population. The *Munich Post* did not mince their words in order to "denounce the shocking events inside the *Hitler Party*". These articles went above and beyond condemning the openly homosexual lifestyles of *SA* chef Ernst Röhm and his band of sadomasochistic thugs, but they also gave a terrifying hint into the 'strangeness' of the sexual practices.

Sex magic is almost certainly what the *Munich Post* is inferring here; the ritual practice of symbolism, intention and orgasms being unleashed at specific moments of energetic transfer and harvesting. The *Munich Post* constantly reiterated the point which Hitler himself made over and over again—that nothing happened within the party without Hitler's knowledge and will—when reporting on these sordid events. Despite issuing accusations of slander, Hitler himself learned much from the episode, and came to understand the power of sexual blackmail, which he later used upon his own enemies (another form of reversed black sex magic employed particulalry by Satanists). One of his most devoted psychopaths, Reinhard 'Iron Heart' Heydrich—whom Himmler had once praised as having 'overcome the Jew in himself by intellectual means'—later engineered sexual blackmailing rituals to deal with uncooperative elements within the German military who were not too keen on Hitler's war plans. These rituals included employing a homosexual prostitute nicknamed 'Bavarian Joe', a pathetic figure, used to make false accusations against General Fritsch in order to replace the conservative and cautious general with military leaders more sympathetic to the Nazi ideals.

This technique of capitalising upon the strengths and methods of his enemies was one of Hitler's genuinely uncanny natural talents. From sleazy blackmail to the mobile warfare techniques developed by the Soviets in the 1920s, Hitler co-opted many of the very things which could have led to his downfall. Indicating that, as time progressed and his power base grew, he was driven completely and entirely by his own will, rather than any ideological mandate he attached himself to. The *Hitler Party* really was the *Hitler Party*.

Sadly, the *Munich Post*'s revelations of the sex magic rituals within the Nazi inner circle was to be the last real voice of opposition against National Socialism within Germany, and with this, the editors and journalists of the newspaper sealed their own fate. In March 1933, Adolf Hitler ordered a 'final solution' to the secrets contained within the *Munich Post* when his Brownshirts completely destroyed their offices and hauled the entire staff to the concentrations camps. Along with them went the first-hand accounts from disgruntled Hitler supporters who were increasingly shocked by the 'ritualistic' nature of how dissidents within the party were slaughtered. Some of these turncoats went right back to people who marched alongside Adolf Hitler into the hail of bullets back in November 11, 1923.

GELI's SACRIFICE AND THE SEX MAGIC OF THE THIRD REICH

At the height of his growing public and political power, Adolf Hitler's half-niece, Geli Raubal—an attractive and spirited young woman—was found dead in Hitler's Munich apartment with a large hole in her chest and Hitler's personal 6.5 calibre Mauser pistol laying beside her. The discovery of her body added fuel to the fire that the Nazis were obsessed with sex and death following a year-long revelation of 'unnatural' sexual practices among party members being published in the Socialist and anti-Nazi media. It should have spelled the end for Hitler's political career, but immediately the well-financed and highly efficient Nazi spin machine was set into action.

This was made easier by the dominance of right-wing police and detectives within the Munich police department, who were in no rush to prosecute the one man many of them held in such high admiration. Police corruption determined by political convictions was nothing new at the time, depending on who was in charge of the police and law courts. In 1930, Albrecht Höhler, an active member of the Berlin Communist Party, received a very lenient six-year sentence for his assassination of German Nazi Party activist and *SA-Sturmführer* Horst Wessel, who wrote the lyrics to the song *Die Fahne hoch* (*"The Flag On High"*), which eventually became the Nazi Party's anthem. By the time Hitler's star was rising, police had learned to offer the same leniency towards the National Socialists ensuring that Hitler would walk free, and the case would be closed, no matter what.

It was now September 1931, and the National Socialists were at the final stages of transforming themselves into a well-oiled and slick political façade to mask their murky and 'unnatural' front line party members' machinations behind the scenes. People in rural Germany were unaware of—or more likely, just didn't care—about the Nazis' reputation of murder and sordid sexuality that the big city newspapers carried almost daily concerning Hitler and his inner circle. Hitler, often arriving to the agricultural and remote industrial regions of the Fatherland by aeroplane (during the brilliantly designed and implemented '*Hitler Over Germany*' campaign), would have been seen—as was his intention—as a kind of Nordic god of salvation descending upon their community from the domain of Thor, with promises of restored dignity and honour, and enemies vanquished. Hitler also understood that these highly conservative provincial communities distrusted the intelligentsia as well as the artists of Munich, Frankfurt and Berlin, and likewise would have also shunned reading their newspapers, thus remaining unaware of the full extent of the shady details of National Socialism's after-hours antics, and even if they did read them, would have brushed it off as "Jewish lies".

Even with this growing support from the hinterlands, Hitler still had a potential political disaster on his hands with the scandal of Geli Raubal's death, which had to be sorted out as soon as possible. While being interrogated by Detective Sauer of the Munich police department, Hitler made a comment concerning his dead half-niece that offers an insight into the true nature of their relationship (if one reads beneath the surface), as well as being designed to portray her as an unstable young woman who took her own life on a whim.

Hitler made the statement that Geli Raubal was involved in a 'spiritualist society of some sort' which held seances contacting the dead, among other paranormal experiments she took part in. According to Hitler, his half-niece was in a heightened nervous state due to one of the channelled voices at the seance, informing her that she was going to die an 'unnatural death' soon. This sensational admission by Adolf Hitler should have set the ball rolling into a full investigation into the activities of the mysterious 'spiritualist' group involved in foretelling her demise, and from this, attempt to establish if they were connected in any way to the Nazi party. Instead, the case was closed and the verdict was ruled as suicide. No follow-up investigation was made into who this spiritualist group was (almost certainly, it was the Thule Society), nor its membership details investigated in order to confirm Hitler's statement to the police. The sympathetic police department wanted the lid closed on the case and, soon after, Hitler was in the clear.

According to servants working in the apartment who were the last to see Geli alive, she had fled from Hitler's bedroom in a highly agitated state before running into her own room where a large 'thud' sound was heard. The staff thought nothing of the noise, assuming it was a heavy book falling from a shelf. Stories also circulated (most likely to be true) that Geli was sexually involved with a young driver within the Nazi party and this had sent Hitler into a violent jealous rage.

At this point, we have to assume that the popular theory which implies that Hitler could have murdered his half-niece out of sexual jealousy may well be just speculation based on what is known as *psychohistory*. Hitler also had an alibi for his whereabouts on that day. However, this is not to say that his will had not been resident within Geli Raubal's psyche, as the image of "Uncle Adolf's" eyes burnt into her consciousness. Did she happen to see who—or more likely, what—lay behind his piercing stare? Later, during the Second World War, the forerunner of the CIA—the OSS—did an extensive psychological profile of Hitler, which portrayed him as a sexual deviant (which is true, but not in the basic 'perverted' sense, but rather that it was ritualistic in nature, and the OSS profilers missed this crucial aspect) and that he had sexual performance problems possibly due to having contracted a sexually transmitted disease during the *Great War* from a Jewess.

We also have to consider that the OSS report could just as easily have been psychiatric psychobabble based on the now-discredited Freudian analysis of his *Sexual Theory* which had gripped American psychology as a kind of hysteria within the profession. This report was, realistically speaking, propaganda employed to de-mystify the German Führer in the eyes of American politicians and military strategists, regardless of actual facts.

The tale of Hitler contracting a venereal disease from a Jewish prostitute was later also used to fuel the single-testicle mythology of Hitler created by the Soviets following the Second World War. Both the Americans and Soviets went to enormous lengths to discard the occult aspects to the point where they became lost in their own compensatory delusions of explaining everything away as merely Hitler's psychology and sexual dysfunctionality, paying no attenion to any occult realities surrounding Hitler and the Nazis.

One thing we do know is that Geli's room in the Munich apartment became a kind of death shrine for Hitler, and he had it preserved to look the way it was at the moment of her death. If we were dealing with a normal human being, this might be viewed as an act of extreme grief, but Adolf Hitler was a proto-psychopath at the very least, and a proto-psychopath or full-blown psychopath's reasons for preserving intact scenes of the dead at the moment of their victim's death is based on reliving the 'rush' of adrenaline they enjoyed at the moment of their triumph over their victim(s). It wouldn't be until 1947 and the publication of Hervey Cleckley's *The Mask of Sanity* that we would be provided with the first legitimate scientific study of psychopathology and the traits of psychopaths, including their ritualistic nature.

This is why serial killers keep mementos of their victims, or return to the scene of their killings: to relive the same 'god-like' *rush* so many of them feel when they witness the life pouring out of their victims. I believe that this was Hitler's motivation for preserving Geli Raubal's bedroom as a shrine. I also suspect that the 'unnatural' sexual acts he demanded of her were very probably sex magic rituals, which were central to the satanic witchcraft of National Socialism. Finally, I suspect that the message purportedly given to Geli—that she would soon die an unnatural death—was not obtained through membership of a spiritualist society as Hitler claimed, but his voice, or rather, this order to sacrifice Geli Raubal was heard within the head of Adolf Hitler himself. His earthly 'true love' had to die, in order for his transformation of the Fatherland to live. The Black-Häxan-Paganism witch king could only love his craft, and nothing else.

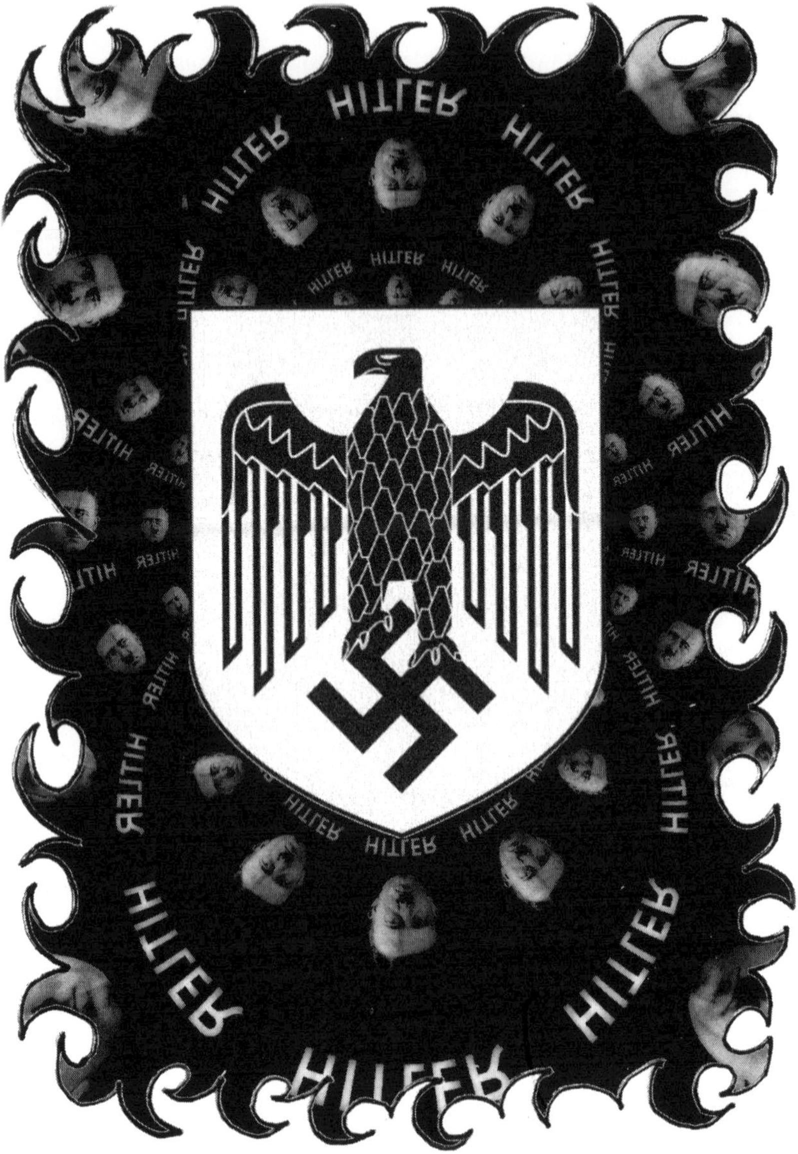
HITLER

THIRTEEN

WILL TO TOTAL POWER

WALPURGIS NIGHT: VOLUME ONE 1919 - 1933

"Sir, your god, your great Bel, your fish-tailed Dagon, rises before me as a demon. You, and such as you, have raised him to a throne, put on him a crown, given him a sceptre."

— Charlotte Brontë

The shooting of Geli Raubal in the heart may also be highly significant, as the Nazis believed that in order to capture the life force of a person or object, the 'heart center' had to be possessed and/or destroyed. The heart was the organ which circulated the blood, and therefore, would have been seen as the engine of the energetic nature of the person or place. This is why Nazis committed suicide by shooting themselves in the head, so their hearts would be uncorrupted. This is also why they shot traitors and enemies in the heart. This even extended to nations and cultures, and why the Nazis so deeply infused themselves with the capitals of the countries they conquered. They were particularly drawn to Paris (heart centre of the Franks), Prague (heart centre of Rudolf II's Holy Roman Empire) and Vienna (heart centre of the Austro-Hungarian empire). Berlin was the heart centre of Germany, and Hitler's desire to possess it more than anything else came with the greatest price. Rationalising the shooting of Geli Raubal as one more scene in his own perverted Wagnerian monomyth, Hitler broke his half-niece's heart in more ways than one. However, the autopsy concluded that the bullet had narrowly missed her heart, so the sex magic death ritual was perhaps unsuccessful in a tragically ironic manner. Perhaps her death set in course actions which eventually led to the demise of Hitler's demonic sorcery? A ritual left uncompleted is the most dangerous magical ritual of all. It will backfire on the magician in time.

Women who became sexually involved with Hitler seem to have all met an unfortunate end. Along with the ritual killing of Geli Raubal, Hitler's previous girlfriend, Mimi Reiter, had also attempted to hang herself in 1928, while Eva Braun made suicide attempts in 1932 and 1935, before being finally successful inside Hitler's Berlin bunker in 1945. Other women who were sexually involved with Hitler who also committed suicide were Frau Inge Ley, Renate Mueller and Suzi Liptauer. Some have even speculated that film director Leni Riefenstahl, another of Hitler's consorts, may have also *killed herself* after being so close to Adolf Hitler; in the form of a life which was one long, drawn-out act of social and profesional suicide following the fall of the Third Reich.

THE BALLOT BOX AND THE MAGIC BOX

As the 1930s drew nearer, Hitler's consolidation of his leadership within the inner core of his own party cultivated a sense of messianic devotion; even to the point where Joseph Goebbels—who, in the early 1920s was unconvinced by Hitler's leadership potential—began writing in his personal journals by 1926, 'Adolf Hitler, I love you because you are great and simple at the same time. This is what one calls a genius.' There were also rivalries among the inner Nazi core to get as close as possible to Hitler, with many being resentful of Hitler's close friendship with Rudolf Hess. In reality, Hess may well have been still functioning as Hitler's occult 'handler' since the days of the Four Seasons Hotel in Munich, while the Thule Society were still running the show with Hess as their go-between. Later developments would only increase the validity of this idea, as Hitler would lose control of his craft when his 'dear Rudi' was no longer within close proximity.

Hitler was now radically weaponising the concept of 'faith' within the Nazi Party as something beyond aspiration, but more as a mandate of the will of National Socialism itself. In 1927, Adolf Hitler told his followers to place "faith in first place and not cognition." Hitler relied on Rudolf Hess to cultivate faith in Hitler to something much closer to blind fanaticism among the party members. Hess created an environment within National Socialist structures, proclaiming that the "founder of a political party is similar to the founder of a religion. He must communicate to his listeners an apodictic faith. Only then can the mass of followers be led where they should be led."

Hess was clearly outlining his occult philosophy on which Hitler's public persona stood. Fully aware that Hitler's success to date was due to his cult leadership, Hess went on to state that National Socialists, and especially Hitler himself, "must not weigh up the pros and cons like an academic, he must never leave his listeners the freedom to think something else is right." This is Hess making the admission that Hitler and the Nazis must listen to their intuition and act upon it immediately. However, their intuition was a trap which had been set by Hess and the Thule Society. It was an intuition walled in on all sides by the National Socialist ideology outlined within the pages of *Mein Kampf*. For their faith, echoing Heidegger's philosophy that only by committing one's self to their own national identity and culture and abiding by it completely could an authentic life be lived, the Nazis offered Germans what Ernest Becker, the 1974 Pulitzer Prize-winning author, termed a "secure communal ideology of redemption."

REAL POLITICS

As Hitler's speaking ban across Germany was being lifted piecemeal from region to region, the Nazis managed to attain a membership of 100,000 active party members by 1928. They were still considered too small a political movement to seem capable of seizing national power via democratic means alone, gaining only 2.8% of the vote in the 1928 elections. However, both Goebbels and Göring won influential seats in central government, in which they openly declared that they would use the 'stupidity of democracy' to clean out the dung heap within the Reichstag.

Despite their small showing in the polls, some in Germany were concerned that the National Socialists were tapping into something within the German psyche that went beyond politics and economics, resulting in the then German Foreign Minister Gustav Strassman, who, upon having met and spoken to Hitler personally, was left disturbed by the encounter. "Hitler possesses a devilish rhetoric. He has an instinct for mass psychology." Vowing to remove Hitler from power, Strassmann suddenly dropped dead from a stroke only hours before the *Wall Street Crash* of October 3, 1929. This event gave Hitler the last and most effective opportunity he needed to captivate all of Germany with his "devilish rhetoric."

THE WITCH KING HAS COME

Between 1929 and the elections of 1932, tens of millions of Germans walked away from their previous political affiliations and even turned their backs on the religions they were raised within, in order to devote themselves to Adolf Hitler. A major part of this seduction of the masses was based upon what we would today call 'reframing' or 'Neuro-Linguistic programming (NLP) techniques, which come directly out of occult circles. Hitler and Hess were the first politicians to make effective use of changing language in order to hide subconscious instructions given to the listener in a manner which makes the underlying concept less challenging and more acceptable.

In this case, a 'positive' version of National Socialism was put into place, in which racism is not actually racism *per se*, but rather, a belief in natural orders that a 'National Community' of racially pure Germans is not borne out of hatred, but by common sense and good science. This drip-feed racism was more palatable to most Germans than the overt hatred of the early years of National Socialism. The "racial tuberculosis" of 1919 was now legitimised by good social and scientific sense, which would be for the benefit of all; both German and non German alike. The hatred was now reframed as a peaceful resolution. Once you were of Aryan heritage, that is.

THE ARCHITECT OF THE TEMPLE

Albert Speer, who would eventually go on to be the Third Reich's Minister of Armaments and War Production, remarked in his biography that upon hearing Adolf Hitler for the first time, he was so deeply moved—by what he compared to a spiritual experience—that he went for a long walk into the darkest part of a pine forest. While inside a grove within the woods of his Black-Häxan-Pagan ancestors, Albert Speer described his experience as "something swooped me off the ground...and beamed a host of alien forces upon me". Speer came to instantly see Adolf Hitler as the man who was channelling the entire German experience—past, present and future—into speeches that required no analysing; just conviction on behalf of the listener. Speer chose to become a 'follower' of Hitler before officially joining the Nazi Party in January 1931.

As the economic deterioration of everyday life in Germany continued in the wake of the *Wall Street Crash* with over six million Germans unemployed, the main bank, Dante-Bank, collapsed, bringing millions of middle-class Germans into the same level of destitution as their fellow working-class citizens. This was the opportunity that Hitler took advantage of to deliver his speeches to the masses with all the carefully crafted word spells and dramatic delivery needed to bring both himself and his 'knights' to the round table of German leadership. With a growing coterie of intellectuals, scientists, business people and celebrities endorsing Adolf Hitler, the National Socialists became the only realistic option that the German middle classes could support. Regarding their anti-Semitism, many educated and middle-class Germans naively assured their Jewish friends and workmates that it was only the 'Jews in the East' that the Nazis were concerned about, and not German Jews. At this point, Germans were placing spells upon themselves as desperate rationalisations as to why they had to support Hitler and the Nazis. This was the point where Nazi magic became a form of perpetual motion of agency, as the rotating hammers of Thor placed within the psyche of the German population beat their own salvation into compliance with Hitler's will.

Hitler, Hess and Goebbels now worked together to craft the persona of Adolf Hitler as Germany's last chance. All the tricks and techniques of the 'craft' would be called upon now, as the psyche of the German masses were at their most vulnerable and in desperate need of salvation. Astrological charts and predictions were consulted as to when Hitler should deliver specific speeches on certain topics, as well as the manner in which these speeches were to be delivered.

They employed a mysterious figure from within Munich occult circles named Erik Jan Hanussen to coach Hitler into a more dynamic and wizard-like orator. Although Hanussen, who claimed to be of Danish royalty, but turned out to be a Moravian Jew named Hermann Steinschneider from Vienna and very possibly also a Theosophist, reveals an intriguing relationship between the two in terms of what Hanussen was really up to. As well as an acting coach, Hanussen was a practising astrologer, clairvoyant and fortune-teller and, most significant of all, a hypnotist.

Possessing a brilliant and dynamic personality, Hanussen educated Hitler in how to dramatically stage meetings beyond the current level of Nazi events, and also on how to deliver speeches in order to express the most powerful dramatic effect in the style of an actor on the stage. All magical ritual is about building up the energy to a level of absolute concentration and anticipation and then delivering the charge towards the objective. By all accounts, Hanussen developed an amiable rapport with Adolf Hitler, as Hanussen claimed that he came to know Hitler through old occult circles in Munich back in the early 1920s. "There was much whispering of the coming of another Charlemagne and a new Reich," Hanussen later stated.

With Hitler now proficient in the art of stagecraft and wooing Germans over to the National Socialist cause in their hundreds of thousands with each month, Joseph Goebbels was appointed head of the Nazi propaganda machine, and he could now finally do to the Communists and Social Democrats on a national stage what he had already done to them in Berlin. One of Goebbels' first acts was during election campaigns, where he had Hitler arrive in as many locations as possible by aircraft, while his rivals were still at the mercy of train timetables and slow roads. Hitler was often in and out of communities, having already captivated them with dramatic speeches while his opposition were still en route. The rural Germans were especially taken by Hitler's arrival and departure by air, as it reminded them of the myths and legends of their past; knights arriving on the backs of dragons and wizards flying down from the clouds with special magical powers. None of this was done by accident. The Nazis, dressing more and more in black clothing, knew precisely what they were doing. Women were also coming to the fore of the National Socialist culture as mavens, and wise and elegant 'Nordic Beauties', who were given an early form of feminism within the party, and which also attracted large numbers of lesbians who, in time, became some of Hitler's most fanatical and dangerous devotees.

THE DARKENED GHOSTS OF THE GERMANIC SOUL

Understanding the occult history of Germany provides us with so much insight into the deep well of archetypes and folk memories of that culture, and how collectively Hitler, Hess, Goebbels and Himmler used them to such intense effect. A painting is not possible without a canvas, and German occult history was a vast landscape painting of darkened alcoves filled with hidden terrors and elusive monsters. The formal writings of Germanic or Teutonic occultism began in the Middle Ages, as authors such as Snorre Sturluson and Saemund conveyed somewhat historical tales such as *The Nibelungenlied* (*The Song of the Nibelungs*), with exploits surrounding magical and supernatural events derived exclusively from Teutonic folk and oral sources. To fully comprehend the meaning behind these tales, an understanding of the nature of Teutonic folks traditions in needed, which, unlike the Celtic folk traditions, was not based upon holy men and a priest class. In Germany, women were the main practitioners, and where hieroglyphic Runic script or 'secrets of the Runes' were the central focus of their magical rites. Teutonic magic was essentially 'black' in nature, in that it was almost exclusively concerned with curses, hexes and other rituals designed to cause or deflect suffering. So much of Teutonic magic is about psychic weapons and means of destruction to destroy or damage the health and property of others without mercy.

The complicated system of the Runes gave the early women

practitioners incredible powers within their community, and may have even been a counterbalance to the power that the knights enjoyed at the same time. A motif emerges here, of female witches and male knights, with tales of male knights often being cursed by the Runes, leading them to be struck down in battle. The use and fear that the Runes created ran through all strata of Teutonic society. The term 'Rune' is derived from the old *Low German* dialect meaning 'to scratch' or 'to cut into'. Later on, the mysteries of the Runes moved from the early female practitioners to males involved within the clerical and legal professions. Also around this time, the Runes moved from being carved into wood and stone ("written in stone") to being written into books and on documents.

Even among the early Christian educated classes, the Runes still retained a sense of awe; that in order to decipher their secrets, coupled with using them correctly, they could unleash powerful streams of energetic forces towards their desired objective. As the Rune script became more and more incorporated into the educated classes and further away from the peasants, its power was believed to be even greater due to the decreasing numbers of ordinary folk who understood the potential of the Runes.

This may seem absurd to people reading this now, but this is the fundamental ethos of magic in terms of focusing consciousness towards the absolute and specifically focused will. The increasingly exclusivity of the Runic practitioners as the Middle Ages progressed would have allowed the people in possession of the secrets of the Runes to develop powerful levels of concentration and psychic force. In those times, the Runes were not used for script in a manner similar to, say, hieroglyphics. They were used more as markings to infuse objects such as swords, axes, tools and personal objects such as jewellery and even furniture with supernatural power. Now think of the Runic regalia and insignia on Nazi uniforms and a true picture begins to emerge as to why they were adopted and placed into use. The Runes on Nazi uniforms and equipment was not for standardised graphic design reasons alone. It was magical technology.

The letters of the Runic alphabet, or *Futhorc*, are symbolic in nature, representing animals, trees, and both natural and man-made objects. The origin of the word 'spell' comes from the actual act of making an incision into the wood or stone in order to form the Runic letter. The Runes also allowed humans—if the Runes were used properly—to call upon assistance from nature spirits or to summon demons. Dwarfs, elven, trolls and undines could be contacted in this manner, and even be enslaved for human purposes. The association of these non-human beings and the mountains was also very significant, and within their underground lairs, the dwarfs could be employed to create magical (wonder) weapons which could provide invisibility to human warriors and possess super-human strength.

This idea becomes psychologically and esoterically very interesting, as the Nazis were constantly building underground operation bases, or developing their super-weapons such as the *V1* and *V2* rockets inside mountains. The Nazi war machine itself—following the invasion of Russia—was controlled and developed from secret bunkers under the ground and inside mountains. Covens inside caverns.

In the northern Teutonic magical tradition, the central ritual was the 'raising of storms', and the veneration of knotted rope brought over from Scandinavia—mostly Finnish in origin—which the Germanic people sought at times of salvation and war. It is worth noting here that the Finns were Germany's allies during the war and fought alongside German '*Storm*troopers'. Magical transformation from humans into powerful animals as a means to possess their powers of hunting and camouflaging themselves was why the Nazi military machine eventually named their tanks 'Tiger', 'Leopard' and 'Panther'. The Nazi obsession with blood may also have had its roots in this period of Teutonic magic, as the German witch—the Hexe—was a vampire who lived on blood.

THE RIDE OF THE VALKYRIE

Among the Häxan, the witch class of the Germans, great festivals were held during the Witches' Sabbath, and once again (along with underground conclaves), we see an emphasis on mountains and visitations to kings living in mountain domains. Adolf Hitler's eventual home was the *Berghof* in the Bavarian Alps, where his generals and officials came to visit him for orders and instructions. The Valkyries (from the Old Norse, *Valkyrja*, meaning 'chooser of the slain,) were the classic flying witches on broomsticks, flying in squadrons and terrorising Christians with lightening storms and tempests striking fear into the hearts of all with their terrifying screams. Now consider this in the context of the Luftwaffe's *Stuka* Dive Bombers at the head of the German military *Blitzkrieg* coming out of the sky in a near vertical dive attack, with their machine guns blazing and bombs dropping on the targets, while their wailing sirens struck terror and caused chaos on the ground. The technical development of the *Stuka* had it origins in an archetypal folk memory of Teutonic witchcraft. From the days of the *Electronic God* within the pages of *Ostara*, the Nazis would eventually employ machine witches, monsters and electronic demons of their own in time.

THE CLOSING OF THE INITIAL RITE

Utilising the developing magic of film technology, Adolf Hitler delivered the first ever election speech to be shown in cinemas, with speech and sound fully synchronised. The effect this had was nothing short of cataclysmic for the psyche of the vulnerable Germans who watched these newsreels. Offering his "unbounded loyalty" to the German people, Hitler vowed to rid Germany of democracy and bring about a Third Reich, even to the point of offering up his own life during this propaganda film to save five Stormtroopers who had been sentenced to death for murdering a Communist. Powerful stuff indeed, and far removed from anything heard by any democratic politician muttering about inflation and unemployment figures. Here was Adolf Hitler, a Teutonic King, an *Electronic God,* offering up his own life for that of his knights. The fractured German psyche was powerless to his spell.

Having failed in his challenge to take the presidency from the aging Hindenberg, the results of the following July 1932 election brought Adolf Hitler and the National Socialists a massive 230 seats in the Reichstag; with 38 percent of the total vote. The remianing—mainly Socialist and Communist—parties were still in a position to have challenged Hitler by combining their total votes in order to keep him out of power. It would have been pointless and dangerous to do so, however, as a challenge to Hitler's legitimacy would have led to the events of 1919 in Munich being amplified onto a national level. So, as they reminded themselves of what the Thule Combat League and *Freikorps* did to the Red Guards after the fall of Munich, the leftist political parties in Germany stood down and Adolf Hitler became Chancellor of Germany. However, they would wait out their time until the demiurge of *Leviticus* summoned them once again on the May Day after *Walpurgisnacht* 1945, following the Third Reich's *Flight of the Valkyries* to South America and, along with the Nazi scientists, continuing their invocation of the Vril-ya within NASA.

What began in the Four Seasons Hotel in Munich as magical rituals conducted among members of the Thule Society in the years following the Great War had resulted in Adolf Hitler becoming the Black-Häxan-Pagan witch king of the Germans. The magic had worked, and more spells were still to be cast beyond the borders of Germany and outside the fringes of the dark reaches of the Teutonic soul. More importantly, witch kings of other lands were taking notice of events in Germany.

To be continued...

FURTHER READING

The Psychopathic God: Adolf Hitler - Robert Waite (1993)

Hammer of the Gods: The Thule Society and the Birth of Nazism - David Luhrssen (2012)

Explaining Hitler: The Search for the Origins of His Evil - Ron Rosenbaum (2011)

The Jewish Problem – Louis Golding (1938)

Hitler's Pope: The Secret History of Pius XII - John Cornwell (2008)

Our Masters' Voices: Language and Body Language of Politics - Max Atkinson (1984)

Unspeak: How Words Become Weapons, How Weapons Become a Message, and How That Message Becomes Reality - Steven Poole (2007)

The Golden Bough: A Study in Magic and Religion - James George Frazer (1890)

The Invisible Man: The Life and Liberties of H.G. Wells - Michael Coren (1993)

Mein Kampf (Special Banned Edition) - Adolf Hitler (Translator: James Murphy) - 2012

Hitler and the Nazi Cult of Celebrity – Michael Mann (2012)

The Uses of Enchantment: The Meaning and Importance of Fairy Tales - Bruno Bettelheim (1976)